Cover A ceremonial gold glove with silver fingernails, decorated with embossed designs showing maritime-related figures on the arm and anthropomorphic figures with staffs and elaborate headdresses on the hand. The glove is formed in sections joined by tabs; tabs at the ends of the arm indicate that it was once joined to another section. It probably was used on the mummy of a deceased noble.

PERU'S GOLDEN TREASURES

An essay on five ancient styles
MICHAEL E. MOSELEY
Associate Curator, Middle and South American Archaeology and Ethnology
Field Museum of Natural History

Contributor:
ROBERT A. FELDMAN
Research Archaeologist
Field Museum of Natural History

Published by Field Museum of Natural History, Chicago, Illinois

Second printing, 1978

Library of Congress Catalog Card Number: 77-93483
ISBN 0–914868–03–9
Printed in the United States of America

Designed and produced by
Field Museum of Natural History Exhibition Department
Designers: Larry Klein, Elizabeth Shepard

ACKNOWLEDGEMENTS

Peru's Golden Treasures is an exhibition of pre-Columbian gold artifacts that has come to the United States from the Museo Oro del Peru under auspices of The National Institute of Culture of the Peruvian government. The exhibit has been organized by the American Museum of Natural History and is supported by a federal indemnity from the Federal Council on the Arts and the Humanities, United States.

Gold items in the collection were assembled by Señor Miguel Mujica Gallo, Founder and General Director of Museo Oro del Peru. Authorization for temporary export of the objects on display was granted by Peruvian Ministerial Resolution No. 2671-ED-77 endorsed by Divison General of the Army, President Francisco Morales Bermudez on recommendation of Otto Eléspuru Revoredo, Minister of Education; Jorge Cornejo Polar, Director of the National Institute of Culture; and Carlos García Bedoya, Peruvian Ambassador to the United States.

PARTICIPATING MUSEUMS

American Museum of Natural History (Organizing museum)
New York, New York

Field Museum of Natural History
Chicago, Illinois

California Academy of Sciences
San Francisco, California

Detroit Institute of Arts
Detroit, Michigan

ILLUSTRATION CREDITS

Figures 2, 6, 7, 12, 28, 34
Courtesy of American Museum of Natural History, New York
(Shippee—Johnson Expedition)

Figures 4, 5, 15-27, 33, 35, 36-43
Courtesy of the Chan Chan-Moche Valley Project, Harvard University

Figures 31, 32, 55, 56
Courtesy of C. B. Donnan, University of California, Los Angeles

Figures 8, 9, 54
Courtesy of R. A. Feldman, Field Museum of Natural History

Figures 46-49
Courtesy of Maria and Hermann Kern

Figures 1, 16, 45, 46-49, 53
drawn by Clarence Kurdts

Figures 3, 30
Courtesy of Peabody Museum, Harvard University

Figure 10
Courtesy of J. H. Rowe, University of California, Berkeley

Figures 11, 13, 14, 29, 44, 51, 52, 57-59; Plates I - XXXII
Courtesy of the Royal Ontario Museum, Toronto

Figure 50
Courtesy of Servicio Aerofotografico Nacional, Lima, Peru

CONTENTS

PERU

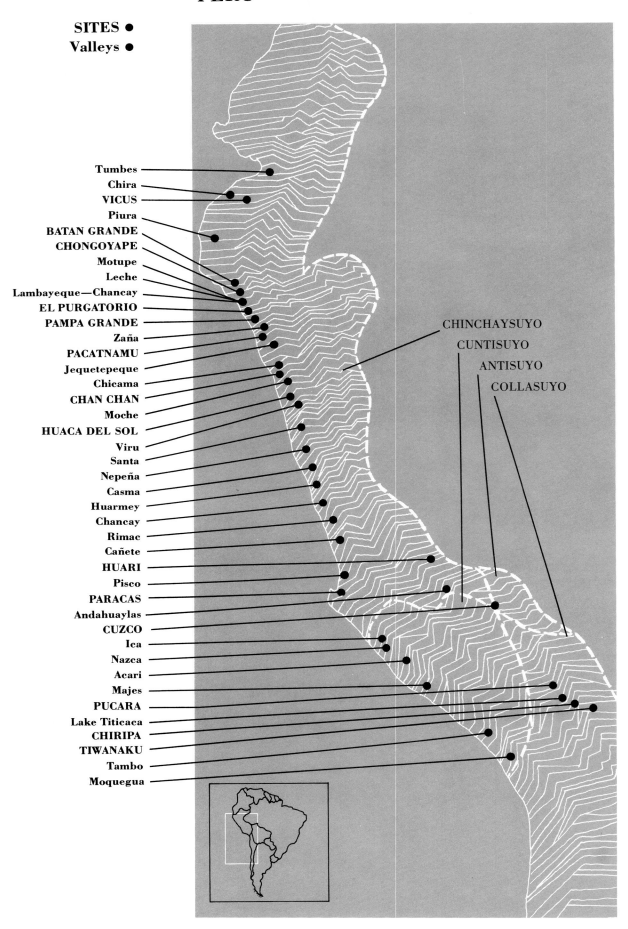

SITES ●
Valleys ●

Tumbes
Chira
VICUS
Piura
BATAN GRANDE
CHONGOYAPE
Motupe
Leche
Lambayeque—Chancay
EL PURGATORIO
PAMPA GRANDE
Zaña
PACATNAMU
Jequetepeque
Chicama
CHAN CHAN
Moche
HUACA DEL SOL
Viru
Santa
Nepeña
Casma
Huarmey
Chancay
Rimac
Cañete
HUARI
Pisco
PARACAS
Andahuaylas
CUZCO
Ica
Nazca
Acari
Majes
PUCARA
Lake Titicaca
CHIRIPA
TIWANAKU
Tambo
Moquegua

CHINCHAYSUYO
CUNTISUYO
ANTISUYO
COLLASUYO

4

I. INTRODUCTION: CHRONOLOGY

The Inca called their sprawling realm Tahuantinsuyo, "Land of the Four Quarters," and, stretching along the mountainous Andean backbone of South America for more than 4,300 km., it was the largest native empire ever to arise in the New World. By dint of armed conquest the masters of Tahuantinsuyo ruled every civilized state on the continent. Inca armies—like their Roman counterparts—marched far beyond the frontiers of Andean civilization to dominate barbarian tribes and heterogeneous societies. To simplify the ethnic diversity they governed, the Inca amalgamated different tribes and states into larger administrative units. Yet, this still left Tahuantinsuyo with more than 80 political provinces, each ethnically distinct from the other. Linguistic variance was equally pronounced and cumbersome, requiring the Inca to impose their own tongue, Quechua, as the *lingua franca* of the realm and the medium of governmental communication.

By A.D. 1500 Tahuantinsuyo rivaled the Roman Empire in its longitudinal extent, and far superseded the size of any medieval or modern European nation. Yet, the might of the empire began to crumble under the impact of Spanish contact about half a decade before the Inca first sighted a white man. Columbus and later explorers moved tentatively and cautiously, but the Old World diseases they injected into America did not. Smallpox and other epidemics raced across the unimmune native populations with fevered speed as deadly harbingers of a new era. Lacking immunity and defenseless, Tahuantinsuyo was wracked by far greater demographic descimation than plagues of Black Death ever wrought in Europe. Then, while funeral dirges still echoed down mountain corridors, a civil war broke out, pitting the remaining populace against itself. In 1532 when Pizarro's conquistadores spread parasite-like into the political veins of the empire, the conquest of the Inca was not beginning, it was all but over. The ensuing rapid fall of Tahuantinsuyo reflected not a victory of Spanish arms or ingenuity, but a triumph of Old World pestilence upon which the conquistadores preyed.

The loot was unbelievably rich. Despite tantalizing finds of gold work from Mexico south, truly large quantities of the coveted metal eluded the European explorers until the conquistadores reached Cajamarca, a mountain town in northern Peru. Here the Inca ruler Atahualpa was captured by trickery. Pizarro deceptively ransomed the monarch for one room full of gold and two of silver. By today's standards for raw gold, the first room was worth about $28 million, and the two rooms of silver would have brought the total ransom to around $50 million. After dividing the treasure among themselves, the soldiers of fortune garroted Atahualpa, and then marched on Cuzco, the capital and heart of Tahuantinsuyo.

The opulent wealth of the sacred city amazed the conquistadores, for there was nothing of comparable magnificence in all of Europe. Among the many palaces and shrines Pizarro's forces sacked, a glimpse of the Coricancha — "The House of the Sun"—is caught in the thoughtful reflections of one Spaniard, Cienza de Leon in *Chronicle of Peru*. Measuring ". . . more than four hundred paces in circuit . . ." the building exterior was of finely worked masonry.

The stone appeared to me to be of a dusky or black colour, and most excellent for building purposes. The wall had many openings, and the doorways were very well carved. Round the wall, half way up, there was a band of gold, two *palmos* wide and four *dedos* in thickness. The doorways and doors were covered with plates of the same metal. Within there were four houses, not very large, but with walls of the same kind and covered with plates of gold within and without, as well as the woodwork. . . .

In one of these houses, which was the richest, there was the figure of the sun, very large and made of gold, very ingeniously worked, and enriched with many precious stones. . . .

. . . They had also a garden, the clods of which were made of pieces of fine gold; and it was artificially sown with golden maize, the stalks, as well as the leaves and cobs, being of that metal. . . . Besides all this, they had more than twenty golden sheep [llamas] with their lambs, and the shepherds with their slings and crooks to watch them, all made of the same metal. There was a great quantity of jars of gold and silver, set with emeralds: vases, pots, and all sorts of utensils, all of fine gold.

Indeed, the elegant wealth of Cuzco and the Coricancha was so great that the narrator felt compelled to conclude, ". . . it seems to me that I have said enough to show what a grand place it was; so I shall not treat further of the

Opposite:
1. Map of Peru showing major archaeological areas and sites.

silver work of the *chaquira* [beads], of the plumes of gold and other things, which, if I wrote down, I should not be believed."

ANDEAN ARCHAEOLOGY

The aims of Andean archaeology are to establish the nature of the myriad societies and institutions comprising Tahuantinsuyo, and then to trace their evolution back in time to the era when man first entered the continent. The tasks are difficult. If a conquistadore felt his eye-witness account of the Inca could be beyond belief, then it is little wonder that archaeologists have problems recreating the complexities of long-forgotten life that once existed in the many ruins dotting the Peruvian landscape.

The Spanish left Peruvian archaeology a mixed legacy. On the positive side are the early explorers' useful records and chronicles describing life in Tahuantinsuyo. On the negative side lies a long tradition of intensive looting of prehistoric monuments. Within 20 years of Pizarro's arrival, looting operations grew so large and rewarding that they were legally synonamous with mining. Ancient monuments were divided into claim areas and titles were registered with colonial authorities. Title holders established chartered corporations, mobilized massive work forces, and systematically quarried the ruins. As with mines, the Spanish Crown was entitled to 20 per cent of the returns, and the returns were great. For example, the Crown established a royal smelter in the Moche Valley, not because of any local mineral veins; rather, the valley had formerly been the seat of the Chimu and Moche empires whose potentates were buried with immense stores of gold and silver. The smelter insured the Crown its cut of bullion from the plundered tombs. Tons of skillfully crafted objects were transformed into ingots, and the tiny sample of intact gold and silver artifacts surviving today derive from more recent looting. Although now illicit, *huaqueros* (grave-robbers) pillage cemeteries at night, while in remote haciendas bulldozers scar the earth searching for deep tombs.

Peru is probably the most intensively looted center of ancient civilization on the globe. One by-product from the four centuries of ruin-quarrying has been the exposure of vast quantities of non-metallic artifacts, particularly pottery. Much of the material was discarded, but a great deal survived as curios and gradually stocked the shelves of museums and private collections the world over. Although Andean artifacts and pottery abound, there is a dearth of contextual information regarding where the objects were found and with what monuments or other materials they were once associated. To contend with the sheer mass of unassociated artifacts, Peruvian archaeology has pursued a strong art-historical orientation in which objects without context were grouped together on the basis of physical similarities and then organized into styles. Because archaeologists cannot compete with the scope of past and present looting, most scientific excavations have been directed at establishing the spatial distribution of pottery styles, as well as their stratigraphic positions in time. Although of considerable chronological utility, this focus on artistic analysis and ceramics has often lead to a tacit equation of pottery with people, and the erroneous assumption that when one style replaced another it was the product of one ethnic group or population replacing another.

Concern with analysis of artistic media other than ceramics, such as textiles and metals, has expanded in recent years, as have studies of food or dietary remains, ancient agriculture, architecture, and settlement organization. Out of this shift to a wider archaeological perspective will emerge a fuller appreciation of the evolutionary dynamics of Andean civilization and its capstone that was Tahuantinsuyo.

CHRONOLOGY

To reconstruct the history of Tahuantinsuyo's people and customs from artifacts it is necessary to organize the prehistoric remains in a framework of time and space. If the original location of an artifact, or the style to which it belongs is known, then the geographical axis of this gridwork is easy to control. The temporal axis is, however, more problematical. Precise dating of individual artifacts is based upon their stratigraphic context in relation to other cultural materials and remains, such as charcoal, the age of which can be calculated by carbon-14 analysis. Lacking stratigraphic context, an artifact can only be dated in relative terms by indirect means, such as assigning it to a particular style. If the internal evolution of the style is known, then the object can be assigned to a particular point or phase of development within the style.

More than 99 per cent of all the artifacts comprising the major styles in Peruvian prehistory derive from looting and, therefore, lack stratigraphic context or associations with carbon-14 dates. This means that the styles they comprise lack precise chronological placement and tend to float in archaeological time.

There are two current approaches to organizing styles in time. First, styles can be sequenced on an assumed evolutionary trajectory moving from simple to complex. But this has its problems. For example, Inca style pottery is generally simpler than some ceramic assemblages produced millenia earlier. The second approach is to employ abstract units of time, called "periods" and "horizons." These units are tied to a "master" ceramic sequence on the southern Peruvian coast, and when one local style replaces another this change demarcates the replacement of one period of time by another. In theory, stratigraphy and carbon-14 can be used to date the style changes in the master sequence and, thereby, the temporal units. In turn, stratigraphy, carbon-14, and trade artifacts, can, theoretically, be used to cross-date styles in other areas to the south coast sequence of periods and horizons.

This chronological scheme is summarized in the accompanying figure. However, it must be viewed with reservations for two reasons. First, the accuracy of the scheme depends upon precise cross-dating of the artifacts comprising different ceramic styles, and such dating is largely non-existent. Second, sequencing is based primarily on changes in ceramics and these have no necessary correlation with changes in other cultural elements.

ARCHAEOLOGICAL TIME TABLE

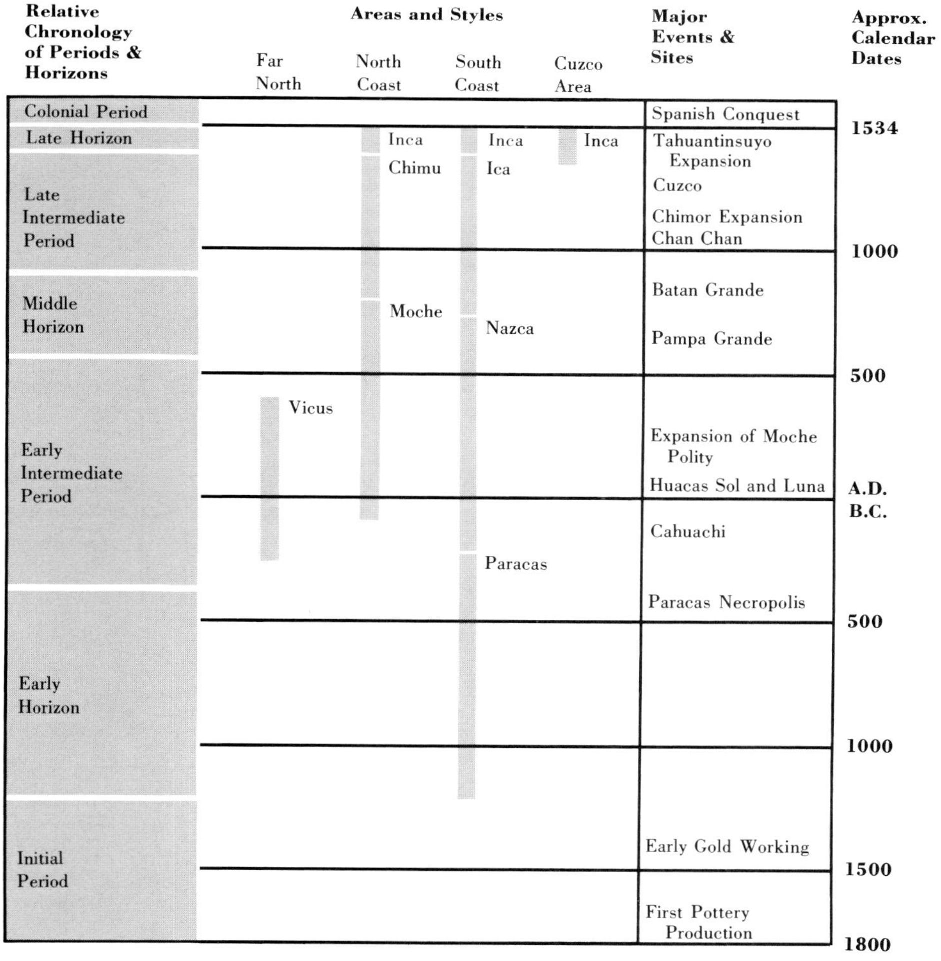

Relative Chronology of Periods & Horizons	Areas and Styles				Major Events & Sites	Approx. Calendar Dates
	Far North	North Coast	South Coast	Cuzco Area		
Colonial Period					Spanish Conquest	1534
Late Horizon		Inca	Inca	Inca	Tahuantinsuyo Expansion	
		Chimu	Ica		Cuzco	
Late Intermediate Period					Chimor Expansion Chan Chan	1000
Middle Horizon		Moche	Nazca		Batan Grande Pampa Grande	
						500
Early Intermediate Period	Vicus				Expansion of Moche Polity	
					Huacas Sol and Luna	A.D.
						B.C.
			Paracas		Cahuachi	
					Paracas Necropolis	500
Early Horizon						1000
Initial Period					Early Gold Working	1500
					First Pottery Production	1800

7

II. GEOGRAPHY OF THE FOUR QUARTERS

The four quarters of the Inca realm stretched over one of the most rugged mountain chains on the face of the earth, second only to the Himalayas in height and harshness. Consequently, geography had a profound impact on the development of Andean civilization, and this impact must be understood in terms of a three-dimensional grid, the axes of which are altitude, longitude, and latitude.

The Andes can be conceptualized as a vast rocky wedge driven longitudinally up the continent's western edge, splitting an otherwise flat land from south to north and forming the mountainous backbone of South America. The stone wedge is significantly wider, higher, and flatter in southern Tahuantinsuyo than it is in the north. However, the lower, more craggy north lands, called the sierra, receive more rainfall than the arid high plains, or Altiplano, in the south.

Viewed latitudinally, the great rocky shim produces a three-fold altitudinal split. West of the highland massif lies a low, narrow, coastal plain abutting the Pacific Ocean. Here rain falls about once per decade, and 1925 witnessed the last torrential downpour of consequence. The coastal desert of Peru is one of the bleakest landscapes in the world, but it is transected by a series of 57 oasis-like river valleys which receive runoff from the adjacent sierra uplands. East of the sierra wedge sprawls the immense tropical lowlands of the Amazonian rainforest. Here there is abundant precipitation, and 90 per cent of the runoff from the Andes flows into jungle rivers.

THE FOUR QUARTERS

Embracing 36° of latitude, Tahuantinsuyo encompassed great geographical and ethnic variation. The four-fold division of the realm was made for administrative purposes, but also reflected salient regional differences within the far-flung empire. One boundary line between quarters ran roughly north-south and another ran east-west, meeting and crossing at the imperial nexus of Cuzco, which to the Inca was the navel of the universe.

Collasuyo

The economic and demographic power base of the Inca lay in Collasuyo, the largest and southernmost of the four quarters. Stretching from Peru through the uplands of Bolivia, Argentina, and northern Chile, this quarter included the vast Andean Altiplano. Most of this great plateau lies above 3,000 m., but a dearth of rain makes it a cold, dry steppe. Man found his most amenable ambient in the region of Lake Titicaca near the Peruvian-Bolivian border. Situated at an altitude of 3,800 m., the lake lies in a landlocked basin some 800 km. long. In the northern part, temperatures average about 7°C., with between 50 and 75 cm. of annual precipitation. While this is the largest expanse of flat arable land in Tahuantinsuyo, its high altitude exerted stringent selection factors on man's economic adaptation.

Subsistence was based on specialized domesticates adjusted to a relatively narrow life zone lying between about 3,700 m. and the upper alpine limits of plant growth. Plant staples included tubers, particularly potatoes, and a grain called *quinoa*. Above the limits of agriculture lie high grasslands, called *puna*, which man exploited through camelid intermediaries: this zone is the home of both the llama and the alpaca.

Although life in the Titicaca Basin is strenuous, the region probably long supported the largest populations found in Tahuantinsuyo. During the first millenium B.C., important monuments were built north and south of the lake at Pucara and Chiripa, and by about A.D. 500 the basin was apparently consolidated under a polity based at the great Bolivian center of Tiwanaku. This Altiplano unity subsequently dissolved into a number of powerful local kingdoms, such as the Colla and Lupaca, which maintained satellite communities on the coast. Subjugation of these polities was critical to Inca expansion because control of Collasuyo provided the demographic and economic stepping stones for conquest further afield in the Andes.

Antisuyo

Antisuyo was the small eastward facing quarter of Tahuantinsuyo, overlooking

2. Ancient agricultural terraces stretching along the rugged mountain flanks of the Urabamba Valley near Cuzco.

3. Llamas served as pack animals as well as sources of wool and protein. This Moche vessel depicts a resting animal with its pack.

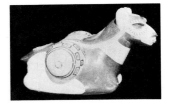

4, 5. Adobe friezes of fish and marine birds at the coastal site of Chan Chan reflect a long-standing interest in the sea.

the limitless Amazonian forest. This province included highland areas west and north of Cuzco, but the dominant geographical feature consisted of the eastern slopes of the Andes, where the landscape falls rapidly from *puna* to lowland jungle floor. The sloping topography is broken by rugged mountain flanks and fast-flowing streams entrenched in deep V-shaped valleys. An unusually high degree of biotic diversity is compressed into narrow, stratified ecological zones that follow the contours of the Andean slopes. These zones created a series of stacked agricultural habitats, each producing plant foods different from the next, beginning with potatoes and *quinoa* at the Altiplano edge and descending to *manihot* and tropical fruits on the jungle floor. The great diversity of resources dispersed along the eastern mountain slopes made Antisuyo a rich region in terms of the types of products available to man. However, the extremely broken topography tended to scatter the exploiting population, and the region never developed a uniform demographic blanket comparable to the Titicaca Basin.

The Inca were fundamentally highlanders, but their economy was pulled into low elevations by the availability of many products which either did not exist or did not grow well at high altitudes. For example, *Zea mays* (corn) can be cultivated at levels up to 3,350 m., but it thrives far better in lower, more moist settings. Because corn was a preferred staple of the lords of Cuzco, it was widely farmed at moderate and low altitudes. *Coca* leaves, from the shrub *Erythroxylon coca*, were another important low-elevation resource. Chewed by people throughout the Andes to releave the fatigue of altitude, demand for the plant led to its intensive cultivation along the mountain foothills.

The tropical lowlands contain many different plants and animals useful to man. However, Inca penetration of the jungle was shallow and rarely stretched beyond the basal flanks of the mountains. Apparently, the masters of Tahuantinsuyo found it easier to draw upon tropical forest resources via trade and exchange than by armed conquest.

Cuntisuyo

The small southwestern quarter of the empire was Cuntisuyo, with boundaries projecting out of Cuzco and cutting the Pacific shore near the Ica Valley and the more southerly Moquegua Valley. The territory included highland habitats, but the dominant features consisted of western mountain slopes and coastal desert. Most years there is no rainfall at elevations below about 1,800 m., leaving the western Andean face and Pacific lowlands bleak and barren. Stratified ecological zones contour along the mountain slopes, but extreme aridity makes them impoverished habitats lacking the biotic richness of Antisuyo.

Although the coastal desert is even drier than the adjacent foothills, people there had access to rich marine resources. Today Peru leads all nations in commercial fishing, an industry based primarily on vast schools of anchovies, and secondarily on larger fish. The schools thrive in a narrow band of ocean currents paralleling the coast from 9° S. Lat. through Cuntisuyo and into northern Collasuyo. These currents support the richest marine biomass of the western hemisphere, if not in all the world's oceans, and for millenia these resources fed great numbers of people.

Streams and rivers were the other main resource complex of western Tahuantinsuyo. With headwaters near the continental divide, these channels collect about 10 per cent of the highland run-off, then cascade down the Andes in steep-sided valleys before discharging westward into the Pacific. Fifteen water courses, about 15 to 35 km. apart, cross the Cuntisuyo desert. Their economic importance comes from irrigation agriculture and large canals that channel run-off onto arable desert lands.

The availability of relatively flat land influences coastal irrigation just as it does highland agriculture. Along the shore of central Peru mountains push out into the ocean and there is very little flat land. Near the northern border of Cuntisuyo a coastal plain emerges, gradually reaching a width of some 80 km. This plain provides considerable agricultural potential, but realizing its potential depends upon the availability of water. Because there is less rain in the southern Andes than in the north, most southern rivers are small and

10

6. Irrigation made the barren coastal desert agriculturally productive. These ancient fields in the Pisco Valley received water from long canals fed by a river carrying run-off from the high mountains.

intermittant and the scarcity of water limits farming. There are, however, several large channels, such as the Majes and Tambo rivers, but they flow in narrow, entrenched courses that lie well below the coastal plain. Even today man does not have the technology to raise the run-off from these sunken rivers and spread it across the desert. Thus, a combination of generally small streams or inaccessible lands circumscribed the economic potential of the Cuntisuyo coast, as well as the more southerly littoral zones of Collasuyo.

The small irrigated valleys of Cuntisuyo supported populations of meager size in comparison to those found in the adjacent highlands or further north along the coast. Yet, these desert enclaves maintained a highly independent and uniquely rich artistic tradition encompassing such elaborate styles as Paracas, Nazca, and Ica. Although highlanders maintained certain satellite settlements on the south coast, and occasionally conquered the region, the desert people displayed marked persistence in local canons and tastes. Perhaps this tenacity is linked to the relatively circumscribed economic base, the limitations of which seems to have restricted the desert populations from competition with the larger, more volatile demographic and political spheres lying to the east and north.

Chinchaysuyo

Embracing all of Ecuador and over two-thirds of Peru, Chinchaysuyo was the second largest quarter of Tahuantinsuyo. Reaching from the Pacific to the Amazon, and extending from Cuzco north past Quito, this quarter probably encompassed greater variation in geography and resources than any other sector of the Inca realm. Likewise, the most sophisticated Andean societies, and the largest states to battle Inca hegemony, had their homelands in Chichaysuyo. The lords of Tahuantinsuyo were well aware of the natural and human potentials of the northern quarter. Outside the region of Cuzco and the Titicaca Basin, the archaeological manifestations of the Inca state have their most dramatic and intense expressions in Chinchaysuyo.

The northern quarter is warmer, wetter, and lower than its southern counterpart, Collasuyo. The geography of the highlands is also distinct. It is broken by short east-west tending mountainchains, and deep valleys. The *puna* exists not as an uninterrupted vast plain, but as long meandering ridges and isolated flat-topped "islands." Man's occupation of the Chinchaysuyo uplands was most intense in the river valleys draining into the Amazonian forest, particularly in the upper elevations near the *puna* . Here the valleys are wide and basin-shaped, and arable land is relatively abundant. With decreasing elevations, the rivers enter trough-like gorges where farmland becomes scarce. None of Chinchaysuyo's mountain basins matches the Titicaca plain in size or population, but, because the sierra valleys are lower and moister, a greater variety of crops can be grown there than on the Altiplano.

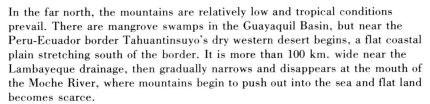

In the far north, the mountains are relatively low and tropical conditions prevail. There are mangrove swamps in the Guayaquil Basin, but near the Peru-Ecuador border Tahuantinsuyo's dry western desert begins, a flat coastal plain stretching south of the border. It is more than 100 km. wide near the Lambayeque drainage, then gradually narrows and disappears at the mouth of the Moche River, where mountains begin to push out into the sea and flat land becomes scarce.

Almost 40 streams and rivers cross the Chinchaysuyo desert, including 10 of the 12 largest water courses lying between southern Ecuador and central Chile. Where these rivers cross the coastal plain, and do not lie entrenched, there are massive irrigation complexes. However, some of the large rivers lie in deep channels, or in mountainous coastal lands which curtail their agricultural potential.

At four points along the Pacific it was possible to interlink canals from two or more valleys to form irrigation megasystems. The largest of these megasystems existed on the northern coastal plain. One tied the Chicama and Moche valleys together. Another united five drainages, the Motupe, Leche, Lambayeque, Zaña, and Jequetepeque, forming the so-called Lambayeque complex, which accounted for about one-third of all the land ever reclaimed on the Pacific desert, and by inference supported one-third of the coastal population. The average agricultural output per unit of land in the irrigated valleys of western Tahuantinsuyo was the greatest in all the Incas' realm. However, the total acreage was small in comparison with the vast stretches of desert or the great upland plains of Collasuyo. Significantly, more people lived in the mountains than in the arid lowlands, but the settlement density was unusually high in the irrigated valleys and the largest coastal populations arose in the northern drainages and agricultural megasystems.

SUBSISTENCE LOGISTICS

The rugged geography of the Andes scattered agricultural lands and other resources among many different habitats, thereby creating an irregular distribution of many distinct commodities among a number of separate physical settings. Most of Tahuantinsuyo's inhabitants were agriculturalists capable of growing sufficient quantities and varieties of food within the vicinities of their homes to be adequately nourished. However, people still wanted items that were not locally available to them. This demand created a problem in subsistence logistics, as to how individuals in one area could obtain foods and basic commodities from other, often distant areas. Trade and exchange networks are the usual solutions, but Andean villagers developed a very different means of dealing with subsistence logistics.

A hypothetical Collasuyo village situated on the eastern edge of the Altiplano would be within half a day's walk of a number of habitats which members of a single family could exploit. The adolescent males of the family could herd llamas in *puna* pastures while their mother and sisters harvested potatoes on the plains below. In a still-lower habitat the father could be preparing a field for maize planting. Activities such as harvesting and planting could go on concurrently because different altitudinally stratified habitats supported diverse crops with distinct growing cycles.

This village would be composed of inter-related families, some of whom worked habitats different from others, and here bonds of kinship led to a pooling of produce. Generally, village lands were communally owned and were not private property, which reinforced the economic unity of the settlement. Indeed, the Inca levied taxes not on individuals, but on communities because they were the basic unit of production and consumption in the Andes.

Although the village used kin bonds and collective holdings to maximize its economic autonomy and exploit the adjacent environments, its members still wanted commodities from localities more than a day's walk away. To satisfy these wants the community maintained satellite settlements in resource zones up to 10 days' trek away. These settlements might be seasonally or permanently occupied sites composed of a few individuals or a number of families, but the satellite was always composed of village members and the agricultural items and other commodities produced always came back to the

parent community. By maintaining a number of such satellites in different distant habitats the community perpetuated its internal self sufficiency and did not need to rely on trade or middle-man merchants.

This uniquely Andean solution to complex subsistence logistics is termed the "verticality" model because altitude produced the greatest resource variation over the shortest distances, and satellites tended to be strung out along an elevational or quasi-vertical axis. Table 1 lists 23 of the more important Andean crops by the elevations at which they can be cultivated. Of these 96 per cent can grow below 1,000 m., and only 22 per cent above 3,000 m. This means that high-altitude peoples require much more access to low-elevation resources than the reverse. Thus, there was a marked downward thrust to the verticality movement.

The model was, no doubt, more elaborate on the eastern mountain slopes where one productive environmental zone successively underlay another. On the western slopes arid conditions created something of a gap between the uplands and the coast, but people still crossed this barrier in quest of salt, fish, cotton, and other commodities. Along a north-south axis verticality would have been particularly pronounced in Collasuyo where the mountains are highest and widest, and where upland populations are the largest. As these characteristics gradually diminish northward, there was, presumably, some mitigation of the model.

The consequences of verticality were many, but the economic autonomy it underwrote in individual communities is particularly important. Villages were not tied by any strong bonds of trade and exchange into large, national economic networks. Because of this autonomy, native states could rise and fall without necessarily dragging the rural countryside into concomitant collapse.

TABLE 1
GROWING RANGES OF PERUVIAN CULTIVATED PLANTS

	Annual Mean Temperature °C	Annual Rainfall (dm)	Altitude (m)
Aracacia xanthorrhiza (arracacha)	15-23	7-15	850-956
Arachis hypogaea (peanut)	11-27	3-40	46-1000
Capsicum annuum (chili pepper)	9-27	3-40	2-1000
Capsicum frutescens (chili pepper)	8-27	30-40	385-1000
Chenopodium quinoa (quinoa)	5-27	6-26	28-3878
Cucurbita ficifolia (squash)	11-23	3-17	850-956
Cucurbita maxima (squash)	7-27	3-27	385-1000
Cucurbita moschata (squash)	7-27	3-28	28-1000
Erythroxylon coca (coca)	17-27	7-40	450-1200
Gossypium barbadense (cotton)	9-26	5-40	320-1006
Ipomoea batatas (sweet potato)	9-27	3-42	28-1000
Lagenaria siceraria (gourd)	15-27	7-28	850-956
Manihot esculenta (manioc)	15-29	5-40	46-1006
Nicotiana tabacum (tobacco)	7-27	3-40	57-1000
Oxalis tuberosa (oca)	12-25	5-25	850-1700
Persea americana (avocado)	13-27	3-40	320-1750
Phaseolus lunatus (lima bean)	9-27	3-42	28-1000
Phaseolus vulgaris (common bean)	5-27	3-42	2-3700
Psidium guajava (guava)	15-29	2-42	28-1000
Solanum tuberosum (potato)	4-27	3-26	2-3830
Tropaelum tuberosum (mashwa)	8-25	7-14	850-3700
Ullucus tuberosus (olluco)	11-12	14	3700-3830
Zea mays (maize)	5-29	3-40	2-3350

Source: Duke, J.A. and E.E. Terrell. 1974. Crop diversification matrix: Introduction. *Taxon*, **23**(5/6), pp. 759-799.

III. INCA: MASTERS OF THE HIGHLANDS

The term "Inca" refers to a small group of kindred, possibly less than 5,000 individuals, who built Tahuantinsuyo by force of arms, and ruled as the realm's governing nobility. The head of this royal family was also the head of state, and by A.D. 1500 his dominion extended over some 6- to 12-million people. These individuals were Inca *subjects*, but they were *not* Incas because this was a closed ethnic caste.

HISTORY

Two centuries before Columbus made his New World landfall, the Cuzco or Huantanay Valley housed a number of small peasant populations that were largely marginal to the contemporary spheres of Andean civilization. Certain of these people with overlapping interests joined together to found a small settlement at the confluence of the Huantanay and Tullamayo rivers. This simple village suddenly began to flower after it was beseiged by foreigners about 1437 and successfully defended by a remarkable young leader, Pachacuti. After rallying Cuzco's early settlers behind the banner of defense, he unfurled the banner of offense for a long series of aggressive wars. These united the inhabitants of the Huantanay Valley and Pachacuti made Quechua-speakers honorary Inca citizens. He then conquered sierra areas to the west and eventually led his armies south, successfully subduing the heavily populated power base of the Titicaca Basin.

People who vanquish other populations often rationalize their acts both to themselves and to their subjects, and Pachacuti's successes pushed his followers into this tradition. Instead of remaining a loose confederation of different folk, myth remade Cuzco's settlers into a single, homogeneous ethnicity, the Inca, who rallied behind their acclaimed headman and patriarch to establish and spread the glory of their sacred city.

The rationalization process also entailed generating a special creation myth for this newly forged kindred and building a religion around it. To accomplish this, Inti, a divine spirit believed to be the essence of the Sun, was elevated to pre-eminence and declared the progenitor and spiritual father of the Inca. According to the new doctrine, the Inca were Inti's chosen "children of the Sun," the emperor was his executor on earth, and from Inti came the command to construct Cuzco and subdue the world as its empire.

In this credo, the Inca had origins separate from the rest of humanity which had not descended from the sun. Although conquest was stressed, conversion was not. There was little distinction between church and state because the political reality of Tahuantinsuyo was simply the religious manifestation of Inti's plan for his children to conquer the heathens begat by foreign or lesser gods. As executor of this plan the emperor was not only supreme commander of the Cuzco crusaders, he was also paramount priest, divine, and a demi-god commissioned by the creator to order the universe.

Inca myth held that before Tahuantinsuyo there was only savagery and barbarism, while in the wake of Cuzco's wars came civilization. The truth of the matter is that the Huantanay region was initially populated by subsistence farmers unfamiliar with the arts of either conquest or civilization. Therefore, the Inca had to rapidly assimilate these arts, adopt principles of organization from more advanced subjects, and invent other institutions of governance. Much more was borrowed than invented, but from whom is not clear, because it did not befit the Incas' self image to admit indebtedness to vanquished foes.

Pachacuti's conquests included two areas which were once Middle Horizon political centers of states that had collapsed long before the Inca ascendancy. One was the sierra basin of Ayacucho where the archaeological site of Huari had been a major seat of government; the other area was the Titicaca Basin where a defunct state had radiated out of the site of Tiwanaku. Therefore, it was possible the Inca could draw on what still survived from the art and institutions of earlier sierra and Altiplano polities. Such things as the Incas' distinctive masonry, use of stone burial towers, and bronze metallurgy probably drew inspiration from the Titicaca area.

While Pachacuti still reigned, his son and successor, Topa Inca, defeated the kingdom of Chimor, the great north coast empire which was the largest polity

Opposite:

8. Built by the Inca state, Machu Picchu was a settlement of the elite. Its inhabitants included numerous religious women devoting service to the Inca pantheon.

9. The cut-stone masonry of Sacsahuaman, Cuzco's great citadel, is distinctively Inca in style. Each polygonal block was tightly fitted to the next, creating a megalithic facade.

10. After the Inca empire began to expand, the imperial capital of Cuzco was rebuilt in the form of a giant puma. The cat head was a towering fortress, the front and hind legs straddled a vast ceremonial plaza, with the tail of the beast shaped by the confluence of two streams.

to contest the Inca. Chimor encompassed the most sophisticated elements of Andean civilization at the time. The splendor of its capital, Chan Chan, made Cuzco look like a rude village of peasant farmers. With the demise of the coastal empire, Pachacuti launched a massive reorganization plan that included fundamental rebuilding and upgrading of his capital to fit its now uncontested status as the navel of the universe.

Chan Chan's skilled craftsmen and goldsmiths were resettled in the Huantanay Valley to serve their new masters. A plan for imperial Cuzco was drawn up so that it would be shaped like a great puma. The head was the massive citadel of Sacsahuaman, while the cat's tail was formed by the confluence of the Huantanay and Tullamayo. At Chan Chan each successive king had built his own palace, and Pachacuti adopted this practice. He constructed his own magnificent quarters, then built palaces for each of his dead emperor-forebearers to fill out the great Cuzco puma. No doubt many other practices were borrowed, but these were recast to suit the needs of the new state, much like Chan Chan's transplanted goldsmiths restyled their art work to the tastes of Inti's chosen children.

STATE ECONOMY

Monetary or currency systems were not used in prehistoric Peru, and payments to the government were not made in kind. Instead, the state economy was based on extracting taxes in the form of labor. The village or local community was the basic unit of taxation, and obligations levied on each unit were distributed among resident taxpayers by village leaders.

Agricultural Taxes

Agricultural taxation was one of several ways by which labor extraction took place. Land was not owned by individuals, but by corporate bodies, such as communities and polities. It was the Inca practice to divide farming areas into three categories of land, with somewhat varying quantities of terrain in each. The proceeds from the first category went to support Inti, other gods in the state pantheon, and ceremonial activities. Produce from the second was used by the emperor for his own ends and those of the empire. The third category supported the local community, and these lands were reallocated annually among the village members according to needs. However, it was the obligation of the villagers to farm the first two categories of land in addition to their own parcels, and both men and women rendered agricultural labor.

Puna pasture and camelids were taxed in a manner paralleling the agricultural system. State herds were larger than those of individual communities because the animals were widely used as sacrifices on ceremonial occasions and for the production of wool destined for state-wide distribution.

The *Mit'a*

Males had a second state obligation: *mit'a*—the draft or labor service. Able-bodied men had to perform a certain amount of government work annually, and this work could entail a wide range of activities from serving on construction projects to military campaigns. A certain number of workers had to remain with the fields, but otherwise the numbers of *mit'a* laborers mobilized, their length of service, and type of work rested with the whim of the emperor and the needs of the state. With millions of subjects to draw from, *mit'a* obligations seem not to have been overbearing nor unduly long.

The *mit'a* gave the Andean state a very labor-intensive economy, as expressed in well-made road systems, sophisticated reclamation programs, and great architectural monuments. The splendor Cuzco assumed is ample testimony to the intensity of the economic system. Thirty-thousand men are said to have labored at one time simply building Sacsahuaman, the puma's fortified head, and thousands more must have worked on the great palaces and shrines of the sacred city. Indeed, as the state expanded and mobilized progressively more labor, expending taxes may have been a problem. Legend says that one emperor issued orders for an entire hill to be moved from one place to another simply to keep his subjects busy.

Textile Taxation

If able-bodied males rendered *mit'a* service, what then of the far-larger labor pool comprised of women, as well as very young or old men who could not be conveniently separated from hearth and home? The state taxed these people by means of spinning, weaving, and cloth production. To home-bound taxpayers the government annually doled out raw cotton and wool, and later collected finished commodities in the form of cordage and fabrics.

Textile taxation constituted a very ancient Andean tradition, and cloth-making occupied more people for more time than any other craft. Many grades of cloth were produced, and weavers ranged from peasants to cloistered women supported by the state. As a highly valued commodity, cloth fulfilled certain socio-economic roles analogous to currency. Army recruits received allocations of textiles, and meritorious government service was rewarded with gifts of fabrics. Among the aristocracy, the quality and decoration of garments served as insignia of ethnic affiliation and hallmarks of rank. The emperor wore the finest materials, often fashioned from exotic fibers, including threads of gold and silver, and embellished with sequins of gold.

Redistribution

Had the tripartite land-tenure system been evenly divided and strictly enforced, which was not always the case, two-thirds of the empire's agrarian output would have come under direct government control in either political or religious guise. A major consequence of agricultural taxation was that it essentially placed the national economy in the hands of the state. How the state deployed and redistributed its vast stores is of interest.

In part, tax produce supported the non-agricultural sector of the population. These people included the Inca, the aristocracy of subject polities, religious functionaries, bureaucrats, craftsmen, and other full-time government servants. Reliable figures are lacking, but it is unlikely that these individuals comprised more than 15 to 20 per cent of the population, if that much. State stores were also used to support *mit'a* workers while they were rendering government service. The army, composed of *mit'a* draftees, classes of professional soldiers, and the Inca officers corps, was another major consumer of agricultural, as well as textile, tax revenues. Along state highways and near the imperial frontiers there were larger storage complexes stocked with food, fabrics, and arms intended for use by the armed forces.

Yet, in spite of many expenditures, the state did not consume substantial portions of its agricultural revenues. To some degree the surpluses were open for redistribution to the masses. In case of famine or disaster, government stores were distributed to the people as need required, and excess taxes served as government insurance against crop failure. In other cases, when local food stocks became sufficiently large, the emperor ordered a general distribution from government storehouses, usually sending the products to other provinces where they were not grown. This form of redistribution — moving produce from its point of origin to a point of consumption where it was otherwise unavailable—served similar functions to the folk institution of verticality. It may be conjectured that if the Inca had pursued redistribution on an intensive and massive scale for enough generations, verticality and village autonomy would ultimately have been undermined, resulting in the highland peasantry becoming inextricably bound into the national economy.

Reciprocity

The tax system was not simply a unidirectional flow of labor and goods from the peasantry to the government. There were wide-spread, fundamental beliefs that the state had reciprocal obligations to the people. Produce from church lands was expected to support elaborate ceremonies in which people consumed copious quantities of maize-beer and food. The state was obliged to feed *mit'a* laborers, as well as the army, which it also had to clothe. Failure to meet expected standards of reciprocity quickly promoted discontent, and ultimately revolt.

A hierarchy of goods was employed by the state to deal with a hierarchy of reciprocal obligations. Village leaders expected more prestigious rewards than

11. This gold Inca figurine depicts a standing woman.

their community's members, while regional leaders received still more valued gifts, and so on up the socio-political ladder. Food and maize-beer were most commonly doled out, followed by textiles. Other crafts-products used to reward labor and services included ceramics, wood work, lapidary art, and metalwork. Here again there was a strict order as to who received what, with silver and gold going to individuals of the highest ranks.

Arts and Crafts

Reciprocity and the distribution of valued items by rank essentially placed all arts and skilled crafts in direct service of the body politic. Artisans were government supported—in political or religious guise—by the Inca or one of their client polities, and artistic production was geared to state ends. As a result, aesthetic canons, design motifs, and technological considerations were largely dictated by the political and religious bodies supporting the artisans, commissioning their work, and controlling its distribution.

This situation resulted in "corporate styles," which is to say styles associated with particular states and their political and religious institutions. In modern society atrophied elements of such styles are still extant. A banner with stars and stripes, an eagle with arrows and an olive branch, or a lanky "Uncle Sam" identify a nation, a crucifix or six-pointed star denote particular religions, while a feline called "Tony the Tiger" carries economic connotations. This was the general structure of Inca art and earlier Andean corporate styles, but they encompassed rich, emotionally charged symbolism drawn from religion, myth, and epics akin to Homeric tales.

In the Andes there were two levels of economic organization: the self-sufficient community and the state-imposed national economy. Likewise, there were two levels of arts and crafts. The basal stratum was composed of folk or village traditions. These tended to be simple, conservative, and very long lasting. Over this lay a stratum of corporate styles, the canons and composition of which conformed to state dictates. The areal expanse of these styles was governed by the extent of their associated taxation and reciprocity systems, and their temporal duration depended on the rise and fall of the state bodies they served.

The great art styles of prehistoric Peru were all corporate styles, but their underwriting states varied in terms of political and religious composition. The textile, ceramic, stone, and metallurgical arts of the Inca illustrate a number of characteristics of corporate styles. First, they can be created relatively rapidly by borrowing from other people, generating new canons and motifs, and then assembling skilled craftsmen, such as the Chan Chan artisans, to execute the new style. In this process obtaining the requisite craftsmen was equally if not more important than originating new design elements. Second, a corporate style could spread as far and as uniformly as the supporting state-implemented taxation and reciprocity. The Inca exploited Ecuador more intensively and systematically than they did central Chile, and elements of the corporate style are more numerous and better defined in the northern frontier of Tahuantinsuyo than in the southern. Third, stylistic unity at the corporate level has no relation to ethnic homogenity, or cultural cohesion at the folk level. The lords of Cuzco imposed widespread artistic cohesion over much of their empire, but this did not reflect any basic rise in ethnic unity among the diverse populations of the realm. Fourth, and finally, corporate styles could collapse as rapidly as their underlying polities. Tahuantinsuyo fell apart rapidly, but Inca-derived artwork continued in sporadic production for many years. This survival was largely due to the newly imposed Spanish economic system which, unlike some earlier conquests, did not entail reciprocity or the systematic introduction of new aesthetic canons. However, in earlier times when one state conquered and replaced another, rapid changes in corporate style could often take place.

IMPLEMENTING POLICY

How the Inca state functioned is reflected in the manner in which newly subjugated territories were organized. A census or head-count of the entire population was first taken by sex and age. There was also an accompanying survey of the new territory, its water supply, arable land, and village locations.

This information was recorded on scale models of the topography, while population statistics were entered on *quipu*, coded devices made of knotted string. Both survey and census data were crucial to implementing the taxation system, and they were sent to Cuzco where reorganization plans were formulated.

Bellicose elements in the population were removed bodily and sent as a colony to some distant, pacified province. A corresponding number of loyal subjects were brought in to occupy the vacated lands. This reshuffling of settlers, called *mitmaq*, was intended to defuse any potential revolts, as well as homogenize the ethnic diversity of Tahuantinsuyo.

If the territory had a developed political network, the Inca generally sought to implement their policies through the existing government. A provincial administrative center was established, usually at the settlement which had been dominant before the conquest. If local leaders were servile, they were kept in office, incorporated in the imperial bureaucracy, and given prestigious presents to reinforce their status in the eyes of their subjects. Sons of leaders were taken to Cuzco ostensibly to learn Inca ways, while actually serving as hostages. The most sacred of the local idols and certain attendant priests were also removed to the imperial capital and served as additional hostages. An Inca governor was appointed to head the new territories, and Quechua was imposed as the language of government. Lands and livestock were then divided according to Cuzco standards, and the taxation system was introduced.

In the Titicaca Basin and along much of the coast these policies were easily implemented because sophisticated political systems already existed. However, many areas of Tahuantinsuyo were undeveloped and often tribal in their organization. The social and economic transformation of such regions required substantial investments and time. In some areas, the lords of Cuzco seem not to have deemed the investment worth the return. In parts of Chile the archaeological record suggests that Inca activity focused on extracting specific resources, such as copper, and was not particularly concerned with social and agricultural reform. Elsewhere in the empire, fundamental reorganization of underdeveloped areas did go on, entailing heavy *mitmaq* colonization, as well as imposing political organization on the native populations. Provincial administrative centers were built from scratch. Although the work was done by *mit'a* laborers, the architectural canons of the new towns and cities were based on Inca tastes expressed at Cuzco. The types of masonry, room plans, doorways, wall niches, building shapes, and civic layout found at the imperial capital were all incorporated in the new settlements. Thus, the phenomenon of corporate style was extended to architecture and urban planning, and making state-built settlements very distinct from local native settlements.

THE ACCOMPLISHMENT

In less than a century the Inca empire rose and fell. Within this brief span Pachacuti launched a rapid series of conquests that gave Cuzco mastery over the greatest state ever to arise in the Western Hemisphere. Even more swiftly, foreign disease carried away a majority of the Andean populace, as the conquistadores swooped like vultures across the landscape. During their short rule the Inca had set upon a mission to unite and homogenize the Andes through efficient administration, economic redistribution, *mitmaq* population exchange, and linguistic unity. The task was half accomplished. If Columbus had made his landfall a century later, or if his followers had not been formidable disease carriers, then South America would have had a very different history.

IV. CHIMU: MASTERS OF THE COAST

The north coast was the demographic focus of the Pacific lowlands, just as the Titicaca Basin was the population center of the Andean uplands. The majority of desert dwellers were subjects of the Chimor empire, which stretched along the ocean from the Ecuadorian border to just above Lima. Chimor encompassed no less than 66 per cent of all irrigated coast lands in Peru, and by inference it contained at least two-thirds of the desert population. It was the largest state to contest the expansion of Tahuantinsuyo and only with its subjugation by Topa Inca did the lords of Cuzco become the unrivaled masters of the Andes.

THE CHIMU PHENOMENA

Between about A.D. 750 and 850, north coastal people began using substantial quantities of black ceramics in addition to their more traditional redware pottery. Archaeologists refer to the blackwares as "Chimu," and use the term loosely to designate the northern populations living in the nine valleys from the Motupe River to the Chao River.

Chimu pottery is neither a unified corporate style nor a folk style but a mixture of both and archaeologists have just begun to sort them out. It includes the Chimor corporate style and several subsidiary corporate styles of polities in the region of the Lambayeque irrigation complex, which Chimor conquered and incorporated. Black pottery was also used in a wide series of loosely related folk styles by a number of different populations that spoke distinct dialects and languages. Thus, whereas the term "Inca" designates an ethnic group, a polity, and a particular corporate style, the term "Chimu" lacks this specificity and refers to some 700 years of black-pottery production, as well as many different north-coast phenomena.

The Northern Center

The Chimu phenomena have two geographical foci. The larger is the northern five-valley irrigation system known as the Lambayeque complex. Although more people lived here than in any other sector of the coast, the region has received little archaeological attention, and most of the information about its native inhabitants comes from early Spanish accounts.

It is not known when the large canals uniting the five valleys of the Lambayeque complex were built. All were in use during Chimu times, but some might have earlier origins. When the canals were operational they irrigated a more than 100-km.-long section of the desert. However, for unknown reasons, the intervalley canals fell into disuse about the time the Spanish arrived. Building these long water courses required sophisticated engineering, as well as the labor of large, well-organized populations. An idea of what was involved comes from one of today's largest reclamation projects on the coast, which entails the attempt to reactivate one of the canals. The work costs millions of dollars, relies on international financing and engineering, uses modern earth-moving machinery, and has been going on for almost a decade—and this work is on but one of the many major Chimu canals!

The Lambayeque region contains more large ruins than any other Andean area, and a majority of the massive monuments are Chimu. The platform-mound complex of El Purgatorio on the lower Leche River is one of the most spectacular sites on the entire coast, but other rivaling ruins include Apurle, Batan Grande, Patapo, Saltur, and Sipan. It is important that there are a number of very large Chimu sites, and not just a single center of disproportionate size, because this implies that the region was not politically united. Spanish sources suggest there were at least five separate polities in the area and, indeed, if the Lambayeque complex had been politically integrated under one single administration, it is doubtful that Chimor could have conquered the region.

Composed primarily of flat-topped mounds, the interesting site of Pacatnamu lies in the southernmost valley of the irrigation complex. Recent research suggests this monument was a pilgrimage center where devotees gathered at the shrine of a sacred oracle to probe the riddles of life. A number of such oracles were scattered through the Andes. The more important drew followers from wide regions and pilgrims could cross political frontiers with impunity

21

when on their religious missions. The aristocracy must have tithed both rich gifts as well as peasant labor to the shrines and their attendant priesthoods, because some oracle centers, such as Pacatnamu, developed into large and impressive monuments. One of the most powerful, Pachacamac, was located just south of Lima. Its prestige was so widespread and its devotees so numerous that even the Inca respected, but resented, the autonomy of Pachacamac. Their resentment was eased by telling Pizarro's brother that the center housed great treasures, thus prompting the conquistadores to sack the site. The Inca's action implies that oracle centers, while basically religious in nature, exercised considerable political influence.

The northern Chimu can be distinguished from their southern counterparts by a number of traits. Folk pottery of the Lambayeque region was decorated by paddle-stamping, a technique in which a flat paddle with carved designs is used to press vessel surfaces and impart a textured design during the manufacturing process. A common vessel form of the northern corporate styles was the double-spout-and-bridge bottle. This bottle form has an enclosed globular body with two spouts projecting from the top that are connected by a ceramic bridge handle. These vessels were made in fine blackware, and occasionally in gold or silver.

The Lambayeque region was the greatest center of precious metal crafting on the coast during the Late Intermediate Period and until up to its conquest by Chimor. A majority of the surviving gold objects from prehistoric Peru come from rifled tombs of the northern Chimu. As the market value for these objects has increased, so has the intensity and sophistication of looting. Batan Grande and other Lambayeque monuments are now scarred by looters' pits as well as by deep cuts from bulldozers probing for buried tombs. Because the metal objects come from pillaged graves without archaeological information, little is actually known about the northern goldwork. Stylistically, there is frequent representation of human beings with outward and upward slanting eyes. Wearing large circular ear spools, these individuals are garbed in richly ornamented headresses that are bowl- or crescent-shaped. These gold objects presumably accompanied members of the aristocracy to their graves, and served as emblems of an as-yet-undecoded system of ranks and statuses.

Corporate-style architecture of the Lambayeque region is also distinctive, and during Chimu times there was considerable emphasis on building large, flat-topped platforms that supported rooms and other architecture on their summits. The mounds were made of earth-fill surrounded by a casing of sun-dried mud bricks, called adobes. A long, perpendicular ramp projected from one side of the platform and provided access to the summit architecture. Many of the monuments are associated with complexes of rooms, courts, and corridors built at the mound base. These complexes are often enclosed in high walls, thus forming a rectangular compound tacked on to the rear of the mound opposite the ramp. The platforms must have served many different uses. At Pacatanamu the oracle was probably housed atop the largest mound, while at other sites the ruling nobility no doubt held court in the summit buildings.

The Southern Center

The southern focus of Chimu development was in the Chicama, Moche, Viru, and Chao valleys. The first two drainages were connected by the La Cumbre inter-valley canal, which had a length of more than 80 km. Built around A.D. 1100, the canal was intended to irrigate lands in the vicinity of Chan Chan, but saw little or no use.

Early in its history, the Moche Valley had been an important political center, but its regency declined shortly before blackware pottery came into general use. The local population was scattered among a number of settlements at the onset of Chimu times. There were two principal sites: one was inland at the valley neck and stretched along the flanks of a hill, Cerro Orejas; the other was Chan Chan, which had yet to assume political significance. Although a fair number of people lived at Chan Chan and at Cerro Orejas, neither community commanded the labor resources to build great monuments, such as those being erected at Batan Grande and other Lambayeque sites. Around A.D. 800 the Moche Valley may have been politically divided, with the two larger settlements being foci of an inland and a coastal polity. The Spanish recorded a legendary list of the Chimor kings which states that the ruling dynasty at Chan Chan was founded by a lord called Taycanamu, and that it was his grandson, Ñacenpinco, who united the upper and lower valleys, before waging wars of conquest further afield. Yet, even united, the Moche Valley has only a middle-range irrigation system capable of supporting no more than a moderate population. Therefore, both Chimor and Chan Chan must have remained unimpressive in comparison with the great Lambayeque centers.

Still, simply uniting the Moche Valley provided Taycanamu's heirs with a competitive advantage, because populations in adjacent valleys seem not to have been politically integrated. Legend states that Ñacenpinco subjugated the coast from the Santa River through the Jequetepeque River, which was the southern component of the Lambayeque complex. It is questionable that this first phase of territorial expansion was necessarily the undertaking of a single emperor. However, the expansion was most likely based on moving first into the small Viru and even smaller Chao valleys. With these areas consolidated, the Santa Valley's moderate-sized population would have been relatively simple to subdue. The Chicama Valley, immediately north of the Moche River, was over twice the size of the Chimor heartland, but seems to have been politically divided and was presumably conquered piecemeal. Ultimately, the same situation must have led to the domination of the Lambayeque complex, but legend states that Chimor's complete subjugation of the northern Chimu came much later, during a second phase of territorial expansion.

The southern focus of Chimu development was characterized by folk pottery with infrequent paddle stamping, and by the Chimor corporate style. The latter emphasized stirrup-spout bottles in which two tubes leave the top of a vessel, then arch together to form a single unified spout. The vessels were often molded into life forms, such as fish, birds, animals, or people. These corporate motifs were expressed in other media as well, including adobe wall friezes, textiles, and metalwork. While gold and silver were important, the real flowering of Chimor metallurgy probably did not come until the conquest of Lambayeque and the importation of northern craftsmen.

Monumental architecture in the south did not concentrate on mound building to the degree that it did further north. Early in Chimu times platforms were made of solid brick, but later there was a shift to use of cobble-fill. Mound summits were generally reached by switch-back ramps running across the front faces of platforms, not by perpendicular ramps. When the truncated pyramids had attendant room, court, and corridor complexes around their bases, these were built in front of the platforms and not at the rear. At Chan Chan there were only two large mounds, and most of the civic monuments were high-walled enclosures with internal buildings used by the nobility and bureaucracy.

CHAN CHAN

The capital of Chimor had humble beginnings similar to those of Cuzco, but the coastal city was founded much earlier, and matured over the course of five

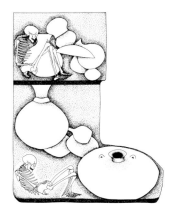

16, 17. Chimu people buried their dead in a seated flexed position, unlike their Moche predecessors who interred corpses in an extended position. The change in burial posture reflects shifting beliefs about entering the afterlife.

18. A plan of the Rivero compound, the smallest of the palace mausoleums at Chan Chan. It is divided into three sectors; the fourth area is annexed onto the east side.

19. An isometric drawing of Huaca Avispas, one of the smaller burial platforms at Chan Chan. At the north end of the mound there is a switch-back ramp leading to the summit. Openings to the summit are from internal cells containing remains of looted grave goods and female interments.

20. A plan map of central Chan Chan as it appeared at its height around A.D. 1460. Buildings are scattered over a 10 sq. km. area. The nuclear settlement covering about 6 sq. km. is dominated by nine high-walled compounds, each of which is named in the figure.

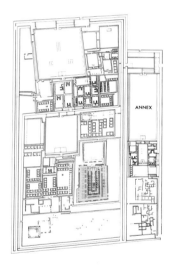

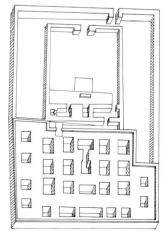

to six centuries. Initial settlement was underway by about A.D. 800, but was neither large nor elaborate. Most of the early inhabitants were no doubt more concerned with irrigation agriculture than with political expansion, and this sentiment probably lasted for several centuries.

However, it was conquest which provided Chimor's nobility with the means and *mit'a* labor to transform their capital into one of the biggest and most splendid native cities in the New World. By the time the empire was at its height, around A.D. 1450, Chan Chan had assumed massive and unique form. The dominant architectural components consisted of nine great compounds, measuring about 200 to 600 m. on a side. In addition, there was a smaller compound, the Tello enclosure, a large platform-court complex called Huaca Higo, two massive flat-topped mounds, and a multitude of smaller monuments and buildings. The civic center spread across 10 sq. km., and outlying structures were scattered over an area twice that size.

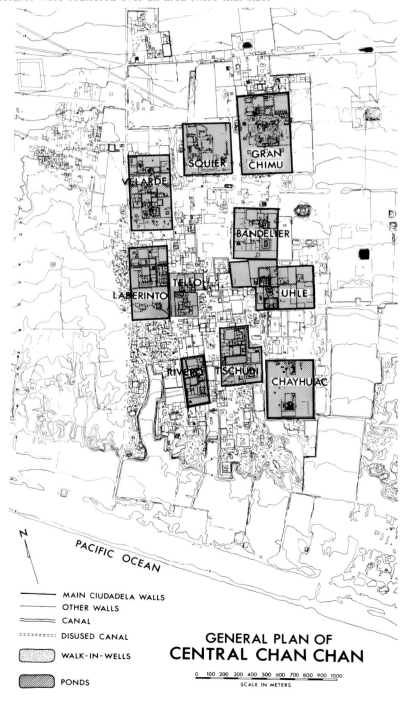

GENERAL PLAN OF CENTRAL CHAN CHAN

I. This Nazca flying figure in sheet gold may depict a stylized bat.

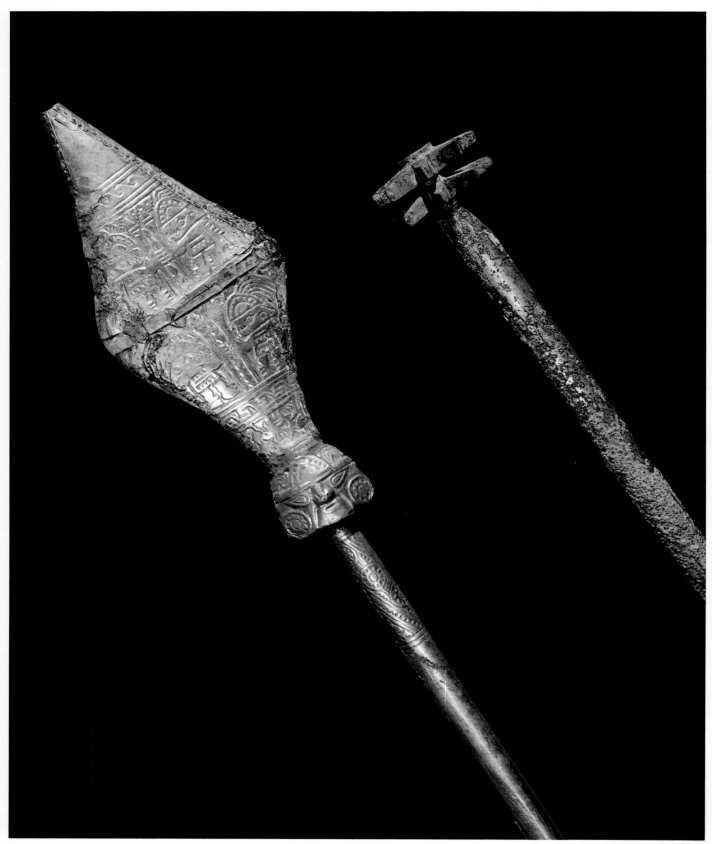

II. Staffs and maces or clubs could serve as the emblems of office. The gold staff on the left depicts Chimu beings holding such emblems. The star-shaped mace heads on the right are probably Inca, but the club shaft may have other origins.

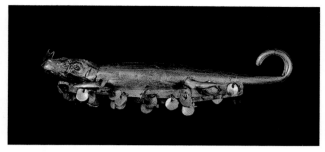

III.   Found in the far north of Peru, this gold lizard may belong to the Vicus-Moche tradition.

IV.   This funerary mask has typical Chimu features. These include upswept eyes, with rods projecting out of pupils, a nose with bangles above an arch-shaped mouth area, and long ears with spools mounted in their lobes.

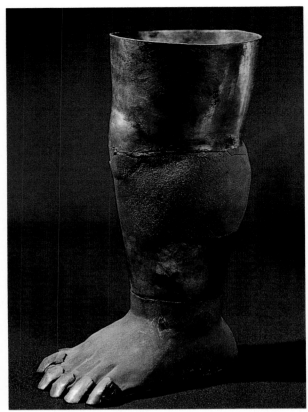

V. Vessels were occasionally made in anatomical shapes.
This Chimu beaker of gold and silver is in the form of a leg.

VI. This Chimu *tumi* ends in two small animal heads, the eyes and
ears of which are set apart by inlays. (Not included in exhibit.)

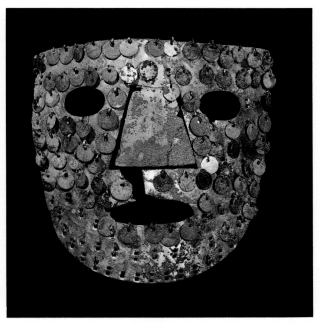

VIII.   This bangle-covered Vicus mask has cut-out eyes and an open mouth suggesting it may have been worn rather than used as a mummy face plate.

VII.   The human face on this gold and silver *tumi* is typically Chimu, as is the headdress which has two small bird pendants.

IX. This detail from the back panel of a coastal litter depicts three figures in Chimu
costume standing in the portal of a small open-fronted building.

X. Representing a human head, this oxidized silver funerary mask has two gold and stone inlaid ear ornaments depicting stylized foxes. This small cheek bulge beside the man's mouth probably represents the chewing of a quid of coca leaves.

XI. This small Inca gold figure depicts a man walking with a cane.

XII. It was a privilege of all adult Inca men to wear large ear spools. This small figurine depicts the stretched-out ear lobes that supported the spools.

XIII. Small Inca figurines of women such as this were often clothed with miniature garments.

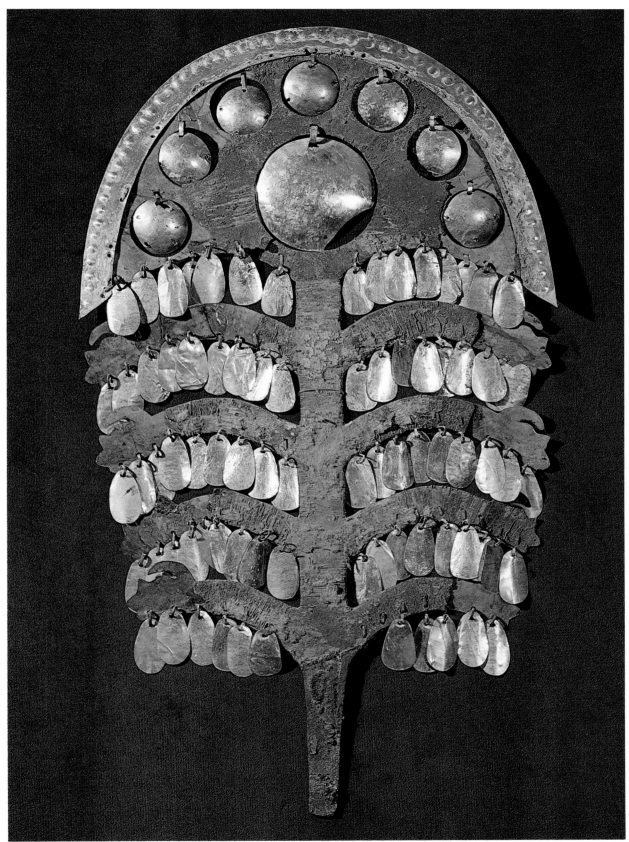

XIV. Possibly part of a headdress or standard, the darker areas of this object were
once covered with thin threads or fibers possibly of cotton or wool.

XV. Made of a copper-rich gold alloy, this Vicus face wears a tall headdress decorated with metal disks.

XVI. This Nazca helmet was made of reeds covered with gold foil.

XVII. Made of gold and silver, this nose mask from the Vicus region is ornamented with a human head flanked by two stylized foxes.

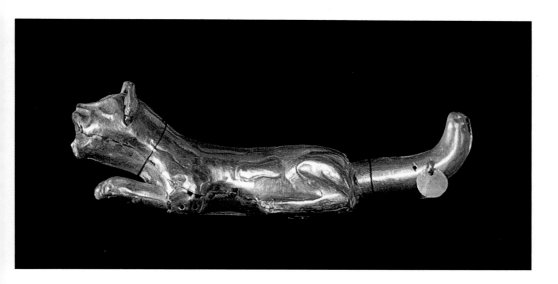

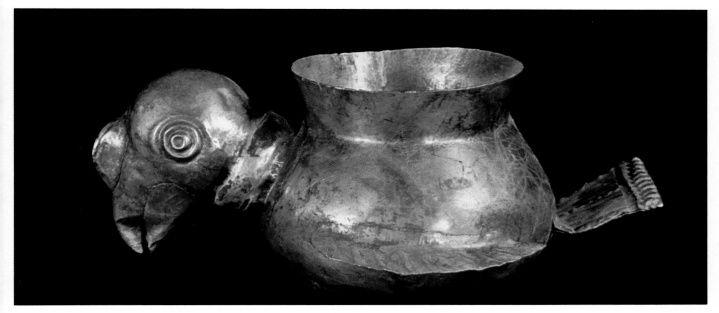

(Opposite)

XVIII. From the Frias area in the far north of Peru, the head of this shawl pin shows a stylized bird mounted on the back of a monkey.

(Top Right)

XIX. This crouching feline, a jaguar, to judge from its body markings, was one of seven identical figures found at Lambayeque site of Chongoyape. Fashioned from 12 separate pieces of sheet gold, the animal dates to Moche or earlier times.

(Bottom Right)

XX. Chimu smiths often depicted animal life in gold work and bird forms, such as this vessel, were popular items.

XXI. Three decorative bands ornament this crown-like cylinder. Birds are common Chimu motifs and they fill the border bands, while stylized serpents comprise the central design panel.

XXII.   Originally covered with red and blue paint this small embossed head apparently
belongs to the Moche style.

XXIII. The nobility often engaged in ceremonial toasting and drinking of maize beer from golden beakers, such as this Chimu specimen.

XXIV. In Chimu times the dead were placed in a seated, flexed position and wrapped
with multiple layers of cloth. In burials of important people, masks, such as this
specimen fashioned from sheet gold, were then positioned over the face area of the
mummy bundle.

(Top Left)

XXV.   Clothes of high-ranking people were decorated with gold and silver. These child's boots from the Chancay Valley are covered with gold plaques and the toe areas are outlined in sheet metal.

(Bottom Left)

XXVI.   Inter-connected double vessels were made in both pottery and gold. This Chimu object comprises a beaker joined to an effigy in the form of a frog mounted by another animal, possibly a dog.

(Opposite)

XXVII.   Ear spools were worn by the nobility as a sign of their rank. In this especially elaborate pair each spool features a modeled bird in the center and long snake-headed bangles.

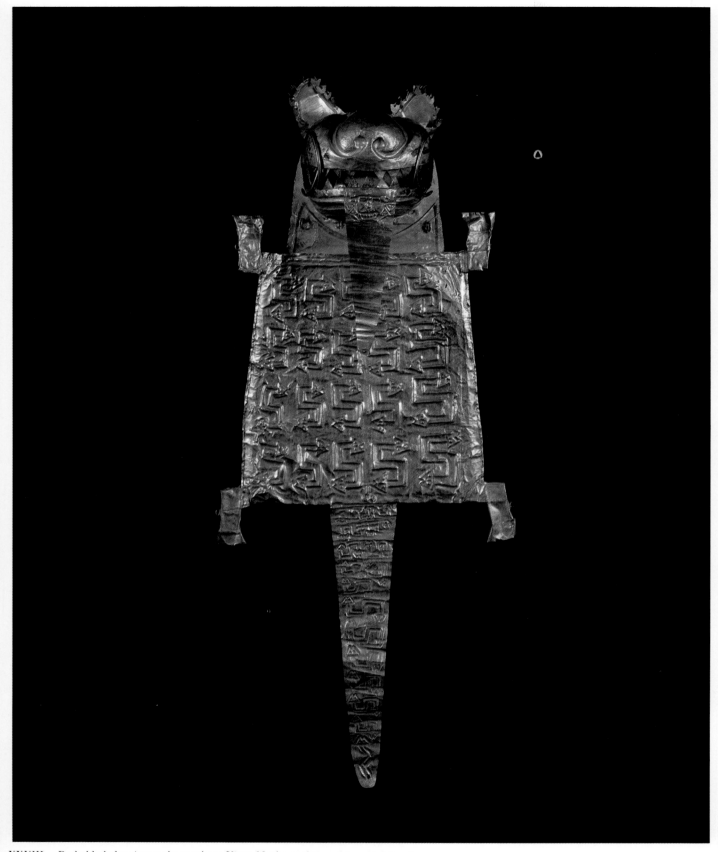

XXVIII.   Probably belonging to the northern Vicus-Moche tradition, this gold feline has
a flat body decorated with double-headed serpents. The head of the cat is embossed in
high relief, with the ears, teeth, and tongue being separately attached.

44

XXIX.   Consisting of hollow gold beads this Chimu necklace carries eight embossed human heads with blue stone inlays.

XXX. Double-spout-and-bridge vessels are characteristic of Chimu ceramics made in
the Lambayeque region. This gold specimen is a copy of the more common pottery
prototypes.

XXXI.   In many cultures hair was symbolized by serpents, as in this Nazca mask of
sheet gold.

XXXII.   Two gold nuggets, an oval ingot, and a hammered-and-cut ingot illustrate the
initial steps of smelting and metalworking.

The Palaces

The nine large compounds, the Tello enclosure, and the Higo complex, were built sequentially and each for a period of time was the administrative center of Chimor. The four major compounds built last, those called Velarde, Bandalier, Tschudi, and Rivero, were erected by four successive emperors. Each compound served as a palace for a ruler while he was alive, and as a mausoleum when he died.

The Rivero compound illustrates the formal organization of the palace-mausoleums. Enclosed by adobe walls two stories high, the structure is rectangular in plan, with an elongated annex on the east. The main rectangle is divided into three sections by high east-west walls. The northern and central sectors have internal architecture; the southern sector where service personnel of low status resided contains only a deep well.

Rivero was entered from the north by a single narrow passage lined with stylized human figures carved in wood. From the entry, a corridor led to a spacious entry court. Most such courts were ornamented with elaborate adobe friezes emphasizing fish, sea birds, and other maritime themes. At the south end of the court lay administrative architecture consisting of storerooms and offices. The storage facilities were comprised of rows of equal-sized rooms, and at the time Rivero was abandoned all the goods in these facilities were systematically removed. Presumably, they were of great value, comprising items such as fine textiles, and perhaps precious metals.

Office facilities consisted of small U-shaped structures, each situated in a little court. These open-fronted structures are elevated 10 to 20 cm. above their court floors. The interior walls are about 3 m. long and there are two symmetrically arranged niches on the inside of each of the three walls. The U-shaped rooms are big enough to comfortably hold one seated person. The structures are called *audiencias* because they are reminiscent of ceramic depictions of small, elevated, open-fronted buildings occupied by a noble who is holding "audience" with people of lesser rank positioned in front of the structure. *Audiencias* are frequently ornamented with adobe friezes, and some had sacrificial human burials beneath their floors. Their little courts sit next to corridors, and one function of *audiencias* was to control traffic to storage facilities and to the interior sections of the compound.

The central sector of the palace enclosure had the same entry-court and administrative architecture as the northern sector. However, there were many more storerooms, and only one or two *audiencias*. In the center of Rivero there is only one U-shaped structure, and it was very likely the "throne room" of the emperor, while the storerooms served as his royal coffers.

The largest structure in the palace is in the rear corner of the central sector, and it consists of a rectangular, flat-topped, platform enclosed in a high-walled court. The Rivero platform is largely destroyed due to commercial mining activities that went on during the eighteenth and nineteenth centuries. Most other palace mounds were also intensively looted, and the best preserved is Huaca Avispas, associated with the Laberinto compound. The summit of this structure was reached by a switch-back ramp system on the north face of the platform. From the mound top openings lead down to rectangular cells positioned around a large T-shaped chamber in the center of the platform.

Although Avispas was heavily looted in the past, recent archaeological testing of the pillaged cells showed that they once contained great quantities of prestigious artifacts, including fine ceramic vessels, elaborate textiles, items of wood, worked shell, lapidary crafts, and metal objects. Excavations produced remains of more than 90 young women, most of whom were between 17 and 24 years old at the time of death. The bodies of some 250 to 500 women would have been found if all the platform cells had been excavated.

These findings have the following interpretation. By the later part of the Chimor dynasty each king built his own palace compound to serve as the emperor's headquarters and royal treasury. He also erected his own massive burial platform, and upon his death the emperor was placed in the central T-shaped chamber. At the same time many young women were sacrificed to

21-23. The entrance to the Rivero palace was once lined with carved wooden figures. The figure shown here during its excavation had a white clay covered face and once held a spear or staff in its left hand.

24, 25. Adobe friezes decorating the Chan Chan palace compounds frequently depict birds in both stylized geometric and curvilinear forms.

accompany the king to the afterlife. In the subsidiary cells he also took with him vast quantities of valuable goods. Included were such tremendous amounts of gold and silver that commercial mining of the burial platforms went on for centuries after the Spanish conquest. Indeed, these were among the richest tombs in all of the ancient world.

The Chimor emperors and their families believed they were the descendants of two heavenly stars, while the rest of humanity came from a lesser set of stars. This creation myth rationalized a caste system headed by the aristocracy. The high-walled palaces were architectural manifestations of this system, since they were intended to physically separate and socially safeguard the emperor from the rest of humanity.

The Artisans

Most of Chan Chan's inhabitants were descendants of the lesser set of stars and resided outside the great enclosures. The minor architectural monuments at the site housed the lesser nobility and much of the state bureauracy. However, the vast majority of the city's residents lived in crowded small rooms of irregular shape, and a cluster of six or eight such rooms formed the quarters for a lower-class urban family. Archaeological excavations in these quarters produced few farming or fishing implements. Instead, abundant evidence of craft production was encountered, including wood-working and lapidary tools, spinning and weaving equipment, and numerous metal-working tools. Therefore, the principal occupation of most of Chan Chan's inhabitants lay in the realm of arts and crafts.

Finely polished stones with angular facets served as metal-working hammers and anvils. Excavations in craftsmen's quarters revealed large numbers of

these tools. They occurred often in family dwellings, indicating that metal shaping, hammering, and annealing went on in individual residences. In other situations, crafting of gold and silver took place in special metal-working shops. Here archaeologists encountered hearth-like furnaces, slag, crucibles, hammers, anvils, and small scraps of discarded metal.

Gold and silver did not occur in the lower Moche Valley. Presumably, mining and initial ore processing went on in the mountains where the state procured the minerals and then brought them to Chan Chan. The precious metals were carefully rationed out to the appropriate artisans for crafting, and the finished products were collected by the state for use by the nobility, or by the bureaucracy in meeting reciprocity obligations. In turn, the state supported its artisans on a full-time basis, supplying the craftsmen with food as well as other necessities, and exempting them from *mit'a* service.

Chan Chan was an unusual city in many ways. It had tremendous size and sprawling monuments, but it was built by non-resident, *mit'a* labor forces. Therefore, the permanent population of Chimor's capital could remain relatively small, numbering perhaps no more than 25,000. The population was also functionally specific, which is to say everyone had a particular job to do. The great majority of the people were skilled artisans. A minority of inhabitants were the aristocracy which comprised the bureaucracy charged with running the state. The smallest segment of the population was the royal family which covered vast urban areas with high-walled palace compounds. However, when the city was at its height only one palace was the active seat of government. The many other compounds were inactive mausoleums of by-gone rulers. In a sense, Chan Chan was a city of dead emperors and live artisans.

26, 27. This drawing and photograph of an ornate adobe frieze in the Velarde palace depicts a person or mythical being wearing an elaborate headdress filled with sea creatures. The birds above the headdress are probably sea fowl.

51

V. MOCHE: FOUNDATIONS FOR EMPIRE

The terms "Moche" or "Mochica" designate a complex archaeological style from the north coast of Peru. There are two separate geographical expressions of the style, one of which is centered in the Vicus area of the northern Piura drainage and is referred to as Vicus-Moche. The second area of occurrence is larger and stretches from the Lambayeque to the Nepeña drainages. Here the term "Moche" designates a tightly integrated corporate style dating between about 100 B.C. and A.D. 700. It is associated with an early polity that employed many of the key institutions which later underwrote the Chimor and Inca empires.

THE STYLE

Moche art is among the most naturalistic to evolve in ancient Peru. From the Lambayeque region south, the corporate style is sharply defined and easy to recognize because it did not originate in this area, and because it replaced a very different local style, called Gallinazo. Moche art was given expression in ceramics, textiles, wood, stone, metal, and wall murals, and canons overlap between one medium and another. There are also sharp contrasts in the motifs and themes of different media, but these are little explored, as more than 95 per cent of the surviving examples of Moche art are ceramic vessels.

Many Moche vessels were made in multi-piece molds and there are two general forms of ceramic decoration. The first consists of vessels with bodies modeled in naturalistic forms of people, animals, or fanciful creatures. This tradition did not originate locally, but was borrowed from either the Vicus area or further afield. Its incorporation in the south coincides with the local development of painted vessels with naturalistic depictions of life forms, which constitute the other general form of Moche ceramic decoration. Vessel painting was basically a two-dimensional type of ornamentation and its canons overlap with Moche style textiles, murals, and metalwork.

Chronology

Moche corporate style ceramics are divided into five chronological phases on the basis of changes in the form of spouts on stirrup-spout vessels. During Phase I naturalistic modeling was introduced, and vessel painting was done using wide brush strokes of red clay pigment on a cream-colored background. These innovations were associated with the replacement of Gallinazo prestige wares, but the traditional folk ceramics continued in use with little significant modification. In Phase II the replacement of Gallinazo was completed, and burials of important people contained only modeled or painted vessels in the Moche style. In Phases III and IV the style achieved a wide areal expanse. Modeled pottery declined somewhat in popularity, but portrait-head vessels depicting the facial features of specific individuals were added to the ceramic repertoire. Beginning in Phase III and continuing through subsequent phases, painting was done with thin, narrow-tipped brushes; the resulting fine-line painting shares some characteristics with Greek vase painting. By this time folk ceramics had gradually evolved to a point where they were distinct from their Gallinazo progenitors. In Phase V the geographic distribution of Moche art changed, and modeled vessels largely dropped from use. Fine-line painting assumed a baroque and cluttered nature with common use of abstract geometric motifs.

Themes

The content and symbolism of Moche art is rich, but difficult to understand. Much of it centers around a set of recurrent themes that are just now in the initial process of being decoded. The nature of these themes is intelligible in terms of analogy with modern beliefs and arts. For example, the birth of Christ is associated with a copious body of lore that is visually distilled in a nativity scene comprising the infant, his parents, wise men, shepherds, animals, a manger, and a bright star. In Christian and Moche art the full theme can be depicted with all its component figures, but more commonly one or another component is used as a symbol invoking the full artistic composition and its lore. Christmas cards do this. Depiction of the bright star or the three wise men immediately calls to mind the full nativity, its religious meaning, and holiday spirit. Many Moche vessels show an individual animal or person and

Opposite:
28. An overview of the Moche capital shows Huaca del Sol in the foreground and Huaca de la Luna lying at the base of the hill Cerro Blanco.

29. Clubs with a small circular shield placed near the center of the shaft or handle are a common Moche motif. This small gold warrior carries a mace and is flanked by two club-and-shield emblems, while a third club is depicted over his left shoulder.

30. A Moche Phase III stirrup-spout vessel combining painting and modeling. The painting depicts a warrior holding a circular shield and long-staffed club with a cone-shaped mace head in one hand. The top of the vessel is modeled in the form of a cone-shaped mace head.

31. This fine-line drawing from a Moche vessel shows a richly attired noble atop a small elevated building. He is receiving prisoners who have been stripped of their weapons and clothes.

32. Women paid taxes by weaving, and this Moche fine-line drawing illustrates the use of back-strap looms.

33. Most of Huaca del Sol was destroyed by hydraulic mining. What survives of the east side of the mound suggests the vast structure was cross-shaped and originally divided into four sections of varying heights.

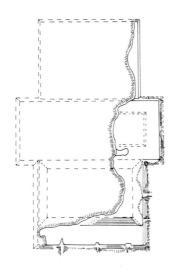

little or nothing else. However, these were not intended to be representations of isolated life forms, rather they are key elements of one or another theme and are symbols of the associated myths and lore.

Analysis of Moche art has just reached the stage where many of its motifs and elements can be segregated into themes, and only a few themes have been fully identified. One includes a complex ceremony involving the presentation of goblets between several sets of individuals. Other themes seem to involve death and burial ceremonies, as well as herbal healing and shamanistic curing.

Distribution

Phases I and II Moche ceramics occur in the Vicus area, and in the Moche and Chicama valleys, but as yet they have not been found in the intervening five valleys of the Lambayeque complex. Phase III pottery is abundant between the Chicama and Chao valleys, and lightly represented in the Santa River area and perhaps somewhat further south. In Phase IV the area of abundant distribution extends south to the Nepeña River, and occasional specimens have been reported from the Lambayeque region. Phase V is well represented in the Lambayeque region south to the Moche River, but it is rare or absent in valleys further down the coast.

The only area in which all five phases are present is the Moche-Chicama region, which constituted a core area for the style. From the core the distribution was first pushed southward, and then northward. However, the corporate art was not well implanted in the northern Lambayeque region until Phase V, by which time it was no longer present in the south.

Because Moche art constitutes a very tightly integrated corporate style, its fluctuating distribution carries a number of political implications, including a state center or core, a southern expansion, and then a northward shift or retrenchment. A number of things are not yet clear, particularly the Phase I relations between the core and Vicus areas. There are also problems with assuming that ceramic distributions are fully coincidental with the frontiers of political influence. Moche-style textiles have a far more extensive southern distribution than ceramics of the same style. Fabrics are well represented in the Huarmey Valley, and occur sporadically all the way down to the Ica Valley south of Lima. It would be logical to assume that both media expanded south at about the same time. Unfortunately, the textiles cannot be cross dated to the ceramic sequence with great precision. In the absence of internally consistent chronological controls, there has been a tendency to suppose the ceramic expansion dates to Phase IV, while the textile expansion was in Phase V, when the pottery distribution was shrinking. No matter how future research resolves this problem, it is safe to conclude that the pottery distribution is largely coincident with the Moche tax and reciprocity system. Textiles may or may not prove to be a gauge of wider political influence and state frontiers.

THE POLITICAL CENTER

The largest Early Intermediate Period monuments in the Moche core area are at the settlement of Huaca del Sol and Huaca de la Luna, and this site is presumably the political center out of which the corporate style radiated. The settlement is on the south side of the Moche River adjacent to a hill known as Cerro Blanco. The occupation area spreads over more than 1 sq. km., and was once much more extensive. It consists of public buildings, dwellings of the aristocracy and lower classes, as well as extensive cemeteries.

The site is dominated by two vast monuments. The smaller complex is Huaca de la Luna (Shrine of the Moon), which is situated at the base of Cerro Blanco and is composed of three platforms with interconnecting courts. The second monument is the vast mound of Huaca del Sol (Shrine of the Sun), which lies near the river. Sol and Luna are separated by a wide plain that is filled with architectural remains. However, the area was flooded in the past and the adobe buildings melted into a consolidated archaeological deposit some 7 m. deep.

Huaca del Sol is one of the two or three largest mounds ever erected in South America, and it is the biggest solid mud-brick structure in the Andes. Today it measures 340 m. by 160 m. and stands over 40 m. high, but this is less than

34. Huaca del Sol (Shrine of the Sun) was the largest adobe mound ever erected in South America. It was both the seat of Moche imperial government and apparently the burial place of dead emperors.

35. This double burial of a man and a woman was encountered near the summit of Huaca del Sol. On the left side of the woman are the remains of more than 30 Moche vessels. Portions of a butchered llama were placed to the right of the male.

half the great monument's original size. After a prolonged period of intensive looting, the Spanish diverted the Moche River against the west side of the structure and hydraulically mined away most of the mound, as well as much of the surrounding settlement. It is not clear what the returns were from either the initial looting or the river diversion. However, the effort that went into plundering Sol was equal to or greater than the labor expended on the larger of the Chan Chan burial platforms, and the Spanish must have been handsomely rewarded.

Judging by what remains of the east side of the mound, Huaca del Sol was probably shaped like a giant cross in plan view. In profile there were four sections, or step-like changes in height. The first or lowest section is at the north and it is likely there was once a ramp here leading to the summit. The second section is somewhat higher; it is also wider than the rest of the platform and gives Sol its cross-shaped layout. The third section is the highest, while the fourth is lower. The early phase of looting cored into the summit of the third section, but not the top of the other surviving sections. Hydraulic mining removed most of the northern three quarters of Sol, but its primary focus seems to have been on the third section, while the rear or fourth division was largely avoided. Thus, the highest part of the platform was probably the most important, at least to the Spanish.

Hydraulic mining left a cliff-like cut through the mound, which has now largely collapsed, except in the second section where the core of the platform remains visible. Study of the exposed architecture shows that Huaca del Sol was built by *mit'a* labor. In planning for construction, the platform was subdivided into numerous small segments or modular building units. Each community work gang was then assigned the task of making adobes and building a specific segment of the structure. Hundreds of communities provided labor, and more than 100-million bricks went into the building process. To avoid confusion each *mit'a* work force impressed a single distinctive symbol or maker's mark on the bricks it produced for its assigned segment of the mound.

Examination of section two of Sol indicates a long building process that must have stretched over several centuries, because the mound underwent at least eight major construction stages before achieving its final form and height. Each stage increased the height of the platform, and, atop each stage, room, court, and corridor complexes were erected. The complexes were used for varying periods of time, during which garbage and refuse were allowed to accumulate on the floors of some out-of-the-way rooms. Then the summit

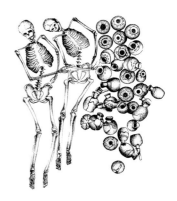

36-38. While Huaca del Sol was undergoing construction, an adolescent burial was incorporated in the building materials. A Moche vessel was placed on either side of the head and the body was covered by multiple layers of cloth.

39. This adult male, with Phase IV accompaniments, was buried in aeolean sands covering architecture in the plain between Huacas Sol and Luna. Traces of red paint covered the skull, and three copper disks the lower face. The man wore a necklace of polished stone beads, and two gold-copper ear spools inlaid with a shell and blue-stone mosaic.

structures were partially leveled, a new construction stage undertaken, and another architectural complex erected on the heightened summit.

Two burials were found in different construction levels. About half way up section two an adolescent accompanied by two Phase III vessels had been incorporated in the mound while adobes of a new construction stage were being put in place. Well above the youth, resting on the final major building stage, was the grave of an adult couple. The woman was accompanied by more than 30 Phase IV ceramics, while remains of a butchered llama had been placed by the man. This double burial indicates that the final building of Huaca del Sol was completed in Phase IV times, while the lower juvenile grave shows that the construction program was well advanced in Phase III. There is no secure starting date for the beginning of Sol, but it may go back to Phase I, or slightly earlier.

The graves also have other implications. The couple had substantial funerary goods, and while the youth had but two vessels, there were also accompanying jewelry and fabrics. In comparison with Moche graves excavated elsewhere, both Sol interments were well stocked, and presumably belonged to at least the lower echelons of the aristocracy.

The two burials provide confirmation of tales by modern grave robbers that other interments have been found in the surviving remnants of the platform. In turn, this supports the proposition that Spanish plundering was directed at royal tombs in section three of Huaca del Sol.

Insofar as Huaca del Sol was the major Moche monument, it seems probable that section three housed the dead emperors of the polity. This argument would see Sol as analogous to the Chan Chan compounds, except that each monarch built his palace-mausoleum physically atop that of his predecessor, rather than spatially separating the new compound.

The three platforms comprising Huaca de la Luna differ from Sol in important ways. The smallest mound and most of the largest mound were built about the same time construction started on Sol. The small platform was never altered, but after very long use the large platform underwent several late stages of reconstruction and elevational increase. Building of the mid-sized mound began around the time of the juvenile interment in Sol, and it underwent many stages of construction interspersed with periods of use. The two larger Luna

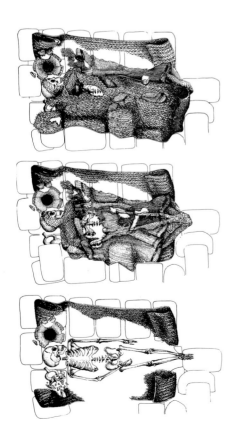

56

mounds were heavily looted and may have contained burials, but the evidence for this is more elusive than at Sol.

Examination of the architecture shows that no refuse was allowed to accumulate on any floors in the Luna complex. Further, the walls of summit rooms and courts were often richly ornamented with polychrome murals. These depict anthropomorphic and zoomorphic beings, some of which share canons with the ceramic arts, while others do not.

It is evident that the activities which took place atop the three Luna platforms were different from those transpiring at Sol. The refuse and lack of murals at the great mound suggest it was the stage for relatively mundane activity. The smaller Luna complex divided its associated behavior among three platforms which were kept scrupulously clean, as well as richly ornamented, leading to the impression that it was the site of more sacrosanct activity.

THE READJUSTMENT

Moche corporate art reached its maximum southward penetration during Phases III and IV when Sol and Luna were reaching their maximum size. In each of the valleys from Viru to Nepeña there was an intrusive Moche administrative center, built in general conformity with the architectural canons of the capital, and occasionally ornamented with murals in the corporate style. Ancient field systems in the Moche Valley indicate centralized administration of agriculture, and similar systems surround the administrative center in the Santa Valley. The Viru Valley center has extensive, but informally organized storage facilities, and there may be similar facilities at other southern centers. Thus the polity based at Huacas Sol and Luna employed institutions governing land, labor, and economic allocations broadly similar to those used by the Chimor and Inca empires.

40, 41. A summit court atop the largest platform of Huaca de la Luna was decorated by a three-phase series of superimposed murals. In the middle phase this head with appendages ending in bird heads was depicted in alternating panels of red and yellow.

42. Dating to Phase IV of the Moche sequence this human figure was used in a mural composition atop Huaca de la Luna. The polychrome composition was painted over several earlier murals, and the upswept eye of the human is a motif widely used by later Chimu artists.

43. For administrative
purposes the Moche state built
governmental complexes in its
subject coastal valleys. A
switch-back ramp leads to the
summit of this platform mound
at the provincial center of
Pañamarca in the Nepeña
drainage.

However, at the end of Phase IV some major readjustments took place. The southern frontiers of Moche influence shrank back to the Moche River. Huacas Sol and Luna were abandoned, and in Phase V a new settlement, Galindo, was founded inland at the valley neck. Its occupation area spreads over more than 4 sq. km. and consists primarily of dwellings, as well as informal storage facilities. There is little monumental architecture at the site, and the principal building is a high-walled rectangular compound. In the rear of it there is a modest-sized adobe platform with a switch-back ramp. The mound center has been cored by looters, and human bones have been found in the dirt disturbed by plundering. However, it is not clear that the structure necessarily contained internal cells and was a true burial platform, like those at Chan Chan, but this seems probable.

The Galindo compound foreshadows the great palaces at Chan Chan. The Moche structure lacks the administrative *audiencias* and formal storage facilities of Chan Chan, but does not represent the center of an empire with great *mit'a* resources. Rather, Galindo seems to represent the seat of local government within the Moche Valley at a time when there was no domination over adjacent valleys. In fact, the local population was probably rendering labor taxes to a far more powerful center in the north.

While Galindo reflects a marked drop in the political fortunes of the Moche Valley, this was just the beginning of a readjustment process that would see the valley disintegrate into several tiny polities at the beginning of Chimu times, only to be reunited by the ascendency of Chimor, which in some ways was like Egypt's new dynasty, arising out of old dynastic roots at Sol and Luna.

It was during Phase V that the Lambayeque region blossomed, and its principal center was the great site of Pampa Grande. The settlement is only slightly larger than Galindo, but, reflecting its political prowess and command of *mit'a* resources, there is a great deal of monumental construction, as well as the earliest known *audiencia*-like structures and formal storage facilities. There are many small platform mounds at the site, but the primary focus of monumental construction was on erecting a single vast mound. In size the Pampa Grande *huaca* exceeds the surviving remnant of Sol and it could well have been bigger than Sol was originally. The platform is of earth-fill construction rather than solid adobe, but it was built entirely during Phase V, which was of much shorter duration than the preceding Moche phases, and the mound represents a prodigious undertaking.

In Phase V the finest Moche ceramics come from the northern valleys, and Pampa Grande was presumably the new center of the corporate style. Although the pottery is baroque and cluttered, it is also thematically simpler, with many, if not most, of the earlier Moche themes dropped from use. Use of modeled pottery also declines to negligible frequencies, and, while Moche art continues in Phase V, its component parts and content were radically altered

to a degree unmatched in earlier phases. Style changes in corporate architecture were equally marked, and the monumental structures at Pampa Grande are fundamentally northern in their canons, ranging from earth-filled mounds to perpendicular ramps. Thus, the art and architecture do not imply that Pampa Grande was founded by a northward retreat of the old aristocracy at Sol and Luna. Rather, the site seems to represent the rise of a new northern nobility which appears to have incorporated the remnants of the Sol and Luna polity, as well as the reciprocity-related art style and the emphasis on building gigantic platforms. However, both of these features were remodeled to northern tastes.

Pampa Grande and Galindo were abandoned at the end of Phase V, when the corporate style also disappears. In the following century northern societies underwent a number of changes, including the shift to producing blackware ceramics. The most significant modification was a shift in burial practices in which corpses were interred in a seated position rather than in an extended, supine position. This change represents a rather fundamental alteration in ideology and it was pervasive at both the folk and governmental levels of society. The mechanisms spreading these changes are not clear, but do not seem to be political, as there was no interregional unity in early Chimu times.

While the transition from Moche to Chimu involved some elusive processes, one fundamental fact is clear. The basic institutions of Andean statecraft and empire were well formulated when the Sol and Luna polity spread its coastal hegemony. These institutions were adopted by the Pampa Grande polity and enlarged upon. With the end of Moche times they continued to operate in the Lambayeque region, and at Chan Chan. Finally, with the rise of the Chimor dynasty, they were further elaborated before being adopted in a large part by the Inca.

VI. NAZCA: SOUTHERN COASTAL SOCIETIES

Nazca is a tightly integrated corporate style found on the southern Peruvian coast. The art has received detailed analysis, and the millenium-long evolution of the Nazca style is divided into nine major phases, which overlap the time in which Moche art flourished. Unfortunately, the associated south coast sites have received little systematic attention, and it is not possible to compare the art to the architectural monuments in a manner that does full justice to local political and economic developments.

The Nazca drainage and nearby Ica Valley formed a cultural core area on the south coast, which at various times exerted influence and political hegemony over the adjacent Pisco and Acari valleys. The southern rivers cross a wide expanse of arable coastal plain, but the mountains to the east do not receive much rain and the drainages are seasonal streams. Most years run-off in the Nazca and Ica valleys never reaches the sea, but is entirely absorbed by inland irrigation, which is not extensive due to the scarcity of water. Because the agricultural systems are not large, the two southern valleys supported only small or modest-sized populations.

DESERT MARKINGS

The local Early Intermediate Period style is in part associated with one of the marvels of Andean archaeology, the so-called "desert markings" of Nazca. The markings consist of lines hundreds of meters long, as well as expansive trapezoids, spirals, and occasional naturalistic creatures formed in outline. The figures occur on stone-strewn plains in desert areas outside the confines of agriculture. The outlines were created by sweeping or raking away the loose surface pebbles on the desert and exposing lighter colored underlying sediments. Although the markings are very long and of vast size, they do not represent great labor expenditures, as the desert stone cover is easily removed.

Creation of the markings required some sophisticated surveying because most figures are so large and are on such flat plains that they cannot be entirely seen on the ground. In other words, their makers could not see the final products. In fact, the markings did not draw modern attention until the advent of aviation led to their recognition and they were then photographed from the air.

There has been a great deal of idle speculation about the manner in which the markings were first laid out and how they could be executed if they could not be seen. Theories have ranged to the point of arguing that Nazca people possessed hot-air balloons which hovered over the desert plains, directing work crews sweeping away pebbles. However, even the most intricate figures could be easily executed by first drawing them on small-scale grids, and then laying out much larger but comparable grids on the desert, scraping away pebbles in appropriate design areas. Textile ornamentation is basically a matter of working with figures and grids, and Nazca people had centuries of experience with such systems.

Questions less easily resolved relate to why the markings were made and what use they could have served. One fanciful theory is that the long lines were runways for space vehicles, but this ignores the equally prevalent geometric forms, spirals, and animal figures that represent mazeways, not runways. Another prevalent argument is that the long lines were employed in astronomical sightings. However, the astronomer Gerald Hawkins, who worked on decoding the celestial calendrics of Stonehenge, failed to find any statistically significant correlations between line orientations and heavenly phenomena. Of course, it is always possible that different markings served different purposes, and a statistically insignificant minority may have had some celestial referents.

Naturalistic markings include forms shaped like birds, dogs or foxes, monkeys, spiders, and fish or sea creatures. At least one motif, a killer whale, has very close resemblances to Nazca ceramic depictions of the same sea creature, and it is difficult to find any rational explanation for etching this figure or other naturalistic markings in the desert.

Desert markings occasionally occur elsewhere on the Peruvian coast. Near the

Opposite:
44. Facial ornaments were often attached by piercing the nasal septum. This two-piece Nazca nose mask covered the wearer's mouth with a denticulate arc. Four whisker-like serpents projected from each side of the nose, while four other elements curved upward and inward toward the center of the face.

45. Burials on the southern Peruvian coast were wrapped in large bundles of cloth. These layers surrounding the flexed body included articles of clothing and large, elaborately embroidered mantles.

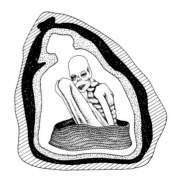

46. This Nazca desert marking is in the form of a vast monkey stretched across a flat plain. Standing on the ground, its creators could never see the totality of the composition they had created.

47, 48. Etched on the barren desert these great birds were created by sweeping away surface gravel to create a path-like outline of the avian figure. Like other Nazca markings, their original purpose remains elusive.

49. This desert drawing of a killer whale is a motif that also appears in Nazca ceramics.

50. The Nazca desert markings took a variety of shapes. This figure, representing a hummingbird, is formed by a single continuous line, possibly a ritual pathway. (Also shown in Figure 48.)

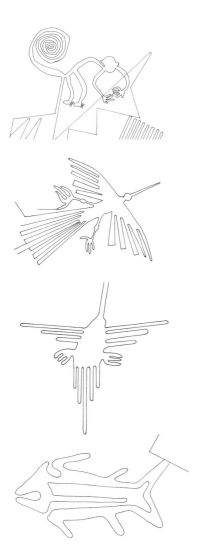

Moche Valley there is a small spiral which leads out the door of a little hut. This arrangement suggests a ritual mazeway in which novices were led from a hut and made to walk a convoluted path associated with some esoteric rite. Although many of the Nazca markings are formed by path-like outlines, they are not attached to little huts. Thus, the use of the desert markings remains just as mysterious as Mount Rushmore might seem to future archaeologists.

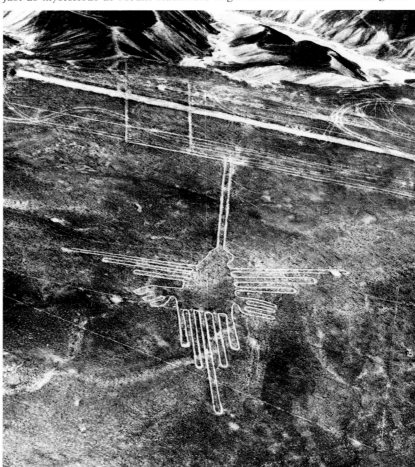

THE ARTISTIC TRADITION

Although the south coast supported only small populations, the people in the Ica and Nazca area perpetuated what is one of the longest-lasting local art traditions in the Andes. It first took shape during the Early Horizon with a style called Paracas. The ceramics are frequently ornamented with polychrome painting applied after vessel firing, but the name "Paracas" generally brings to mind very ornate textiles and only secondarily the distinctive pottery. The most famous site associated with the style is the "Great Necropolis" on the arid Paracas Peninsula.

In the 1920's looters began marketing exceptionally fine embroidered textiles in Lima. The Peruvian archaeologist Julio C. Tello traced these back to some unimpressive-looking ruins that seemed to be a fishing village on the Paracas Bay. In 1927 his excavations at the site unearthed 429 well-preserved mummy bundles in the abandoned dwellings. Dating to the time of artistic transition between the Paracas and Nazca styles, the bundles varied greatly in size, extent of cloth wrappings, and associated wealth. Complete costumes were recovered with everything from cloth headbands to footgear. Many mummies were accompanied by great mantles covered with multicolored embroidery, usually depicting mythical human figures or dancers wearing nose masks and carrying trophy heads. It is questionable that all the graves were of desert-dwelling fisherfolk. Rather, the Paracas Peninsula probably had some special significance that made it a favored cemetery for elite inhabitants of the coastal valleys.

The transition to the Nazca style was a gradual one without any disruption of local traditions. The initial phases of the style are associated with a large Nazca Valley settlement, Cahuachi, which has a number of both small and modest-sized mounds, as well as dwellings, refuse deposits, and cemeteries. The residents of this settlement seem to have been the instigators of a military occupation of the Acari Valley and the appearance of fortified sites in the region. They may also have fostered the introduction of the Nazca style into the Ica Valley. However, both Cahuachi and its associated Acari forts were abandoned in the third ceramic phase. The style continued to flourish at other Nazca and Ica settlements, but in what political contexts is not clear.

The archaeological record indicates close contacts between the south coast and adjacent highlands. Interchange began in Paracas times and continued thereafter. Some of the interchange no doubt relates to verticality and sierra people coming down to the coast for commodities such as salt, cotton, and *coca*. During the seventh ceramic phase a good deal of coastal artistic influence began to register in the highland Ayacucho Basin, where the Middle Horizon Huari polity was to arise. Coastal input continued beyond the founding of Huari and the formulation of the highland corporate style, which is thought to reflect the elaboration of a new religious system. Although the Huari state overran the south coast, long prior contact with the Ayacucho region seems to have mitigated much of the conquest's impact. With the collapse of Huari, the southern tradition reasserted itself in a new style called Ica. This ceramic style persisted up to the Inca conquest, when it was partially submerged by Cuzco influence. However, with the collapse of Tahuantinsuyo the Ica style was revived and perpetuated into the Colonial Period.

In the course of almost three millenia, the artistic tradition that began with Paracas persisted with remarkably tenacity through the Nazca and Ica eras, both of which were subject to periods of highland domination. No other Andean area reflects such long-lasting and distinctive artistic continuity. That this took place in two small valleys with only very modest-sized populations seems remarkable. Yet, the roots of continuity may lay in this smallness. The southern valleys never had the economic potential or population size to seriously challenge the great demographic and political spheres of either the southern Altiplano or north coast. By lying in a marginal position to these far larger centers, Nazca and Ica may have avoided the upheavals and discontinuities accompanying the rise and fall of the great empires.

VII. VICUS: THE FAR NORTH

Vicus designates an area of the Piura Basin, somewhat inland from the river mouth, where in the last several decades looters have found a series of cemeteries with deep graves containing several types of pottery and a variety of metal art objects. A great deal of material has come out of the Vicus cemeteries, but less than a dozen graves have been found by archaeologists, and little systematic work has been done on associated settlements. Therefore, outside of looted art objects, there is very little information on Vicus.

The original Vicus cemetery is rumored to have been found in 1961 by farmers plowing fields. An attempt was made to keep the location secret and in the same year a previously unknown category of ceramics began to appear on the Lima antiquities market. This pottery has been called Vicus Negative because it is resist-decorated with black line motifs on a reddish-brown background. At the same time, substantial numbers of Moche Phase I ceramics also appeared on the antiquities market, and previously such vessels had been quite rare. In addition, gilded copper cut-out plaques, mace heads, and other unusual objects became available for sale.

In subsequent years other cemeteries were found. One which produced substantial early Moche ceramics as well as unusual metal ornaments is Loma Negra. It is rumored to have been discovered by two men and within a few days 800 looters are said to have been intensively plundering the site.

At present it is difficult to tell how the Negative pottery and the Moche wares may relate to one another. They are each very distinct, and one was certainly not directly ancestoral to the other. Looters have said that both occur in the same graves, but this seems questionable. In 1967 several tombs were scientifically excavated. These were 6 to 8 m. deep and consisted of a rectangular shaft with a small lateral chamber at the base which housed the corpses. They contained only the Negative type of vessels and no Moche admixture. Associated radiocarbon-14 assays produced dates falling between about A.D. 200 and 400.

The age of the Vicus-Moche material still remains in doubt. These are modeled vessels characterized by great naturalism, depicting animals, as well as elaborately dressed people. There is little suggesting that this was in any way the fumbling beginnings of the Moche style, and original origins probably lie further afield.

Other than the Moche iconography, the Vicus area has produced relatively little material with close ties to the south. This is in general conformity with archaeological explorations along the Piura and Chira coast lines, which indicates that the area above the Lambayeque region lay outside the sphere of Peruvian civilization until Chimu times. For most of its history the far north was marginal and under mixed influences issuing out of Ecuador and the adjacent highlands. It was first incorporated in the Peruvian cultural tradition by people from Lambayeque or by the Chimor empire when it overran the coast up to the modern Ecuadorian border.

Opposite:
51. This Vicus anthropomorphic mask of embossed gold has carved shell inlays in the eyes, ears, and mouth.

52. The double-headed serpent was a commonly used motif. This Vicus piece has two such motifs, perhaps representing hair, projecting from the top of the stylized human head and a third larger serpent framing the head and forming the base of the pivot.

53. This schematic drawing of a Vicus tomb shows how the dead were placed in a small, but deep, chamber entered by a long vertical shaft.

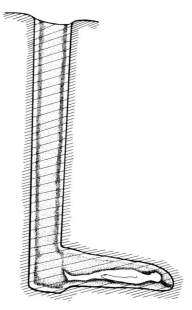

VIII. RETROSPECT

The roots of Peruvian civilization are anchored deeply in time. More than 10,000 years ago nomads first entered the Andes in pursuit of mastadon and other large game, and in quest of wild plant foods. In subsequent millenia there was a settling-in process that called for wide-ranging economic and social adjustments. Economic adaptations to the environmental diversity of the Andes were predicated upon the gradual build-up of a broad repertoire of domesticated plants and animals capable of opening to intensive exploitation radically different habitats varying from highland *puna* and Altiplano to lowland jungles and deserts. Concommitant social adjustments were even more intricate, balancing man with his physical environment, a developing economy, and ever-expanding populations. In this shifting equilibrium lay the origins of Peruvian civilization.

The civilization process began to take hold of central Andean populations between about 3000 and 2000 B.C. Before the rise of irrigation agriculture on the coast, desert dwellers relied on a maritime adaptation to the exceptionally rich marine resources, and the bountiful sea supported a sedentary way of life, population growth, and the rise of large communities housing many people. In this context emerged certain social institutions that allowed a few individuals to direct the labor of the multitudes. These developments found graphic expression in the building of early platform mounds and other architectural monuments of modest size. It seems more than coincidental that the principal craft and artistic medium to arise at this time was cloth. This leads to the supposition that labor, fabrics, and monuments were systematically inter-related at a very early date. The earliest monumental buildings in the Peruvian highlands were erected within a few centuries of their coastal counterparts, and in the sierra agriculture was the mainstay of emerging civilization. However, the nature of early land tenure, and the economic role of textiles in the highlands remain elusive due to poor preservation conditions.

Borrowing domesticated plants from the highlands and other areas, coastal people shifted to a primary reliance on farming about 1800 B.C., and from this time on all of Andean civilization rested on an agrarian economy. There is far more arable land in the sierra and Altiplano than along the coast where water for irrigation is a scarce commodity. Therefore, agriculture supported far larger highland than coastal populations. Yet, up to the founding of Cuzco the very largest mounds and monuments built at any point in time in all of South America lie along the Peruvian coast. This does not mean massive buildings were not erected in the highlands, but simply that a bigger project was generally underway in one or another desert valley.

Comparisons based on the bulk size of monuments sacrifice quality of construction for quantity, and down-play the fact that not all societies or states invest proportional amounts of energy in architecture. However, such comparisons are not valueless in ancient Peru, where there was a systematic and institutionalized relationship between labor expended in construction, *mit'a* taxation, and the size and organization of states and empires. The general contrast between highland and coastal monuments suggests the smaller desert populace was more efficiently organized and governed than the larger, but more scattered mountain populations. It is probably not an accident of favorable preservation that the institutions of *mit'a* and textile taxation, reciprocity related art, corporate land tenure, and redistribution first draw into sharp archaeological focus on the coast with the Moche polity. This does not mean that the system of institutions was a Moche "invention." It was most likely also operative in some modified form among Nazca peoples on the south coast. Although art elements were borrowed from the Vicus region and areas further afield lying outside the central sphere of Peruvian civilization, there is no evidence suggesting the foreign importation of economic or political principles. Rather, the uniquely Andean institutions structuring the Inca and Chimor empires, and earlier Moche and Nazca polities must have had very ancient roots in both the rugged mountains and desert coast.

67

IX. TECHNOLOGY OF PERUVIAN METALLURGY

by Robert A. Feldman

Opposite:
55. Detail of a ceramic representation of a Moche metalworker blowing through a long tube to fan the fire of a smelter.

Peruvian metallurgy has been criticised by some specialists because, in their view, it never achieved the technological level of a true "Bronze Age," let alone an "Iron Age." They would ignore everything it accomplished, and fault it for what it failed to do. But such attempts to judge a culture by a single monolithic yardstick are doomed from the start. First, cultural development does not proceed in such simple steps or in a single line of development. Second, technological changes, as from copper to bronze to iron, do not bear any necessary or clear-cut relationship to social or cultural changes that may or may not be taking place at the same time. Third, such a simplistic view ignores the "fit" of technology to society, whether a new technology is needed, desirable, or even possible given a certain set of social and environmental conditions. A careful and open study of Peruvian metallurgy reveals a sophisticated technology that was, in many ways, more advanced than that of the contemporary Old World cultures.

CHRONOLOGICAL DEVELOPMENT

The earliest examples of metal working in Peru come from near Andahuaylas, in the south-central highlands, where pieces of thin gold foil and the stones used to hammer them were found in a village occupied about 1500 B.C. (Grossman, 1972). These pieces were small, but fairly abundant; analysis shows them to be of native, or naturally occurring, gold. The earliest culturally associated metal objects showing more than simple hammering are found in the Chavin-related cultures of the coast and highlands, dating to around 800 B.C. Most of these early examples are of gold, though it is possible that copper and silver may have been used and alloyed before 1000 B.C. Certainly, alloying of gold, copper, and silver was known by the close of the Early Horizon, when pieces such as the hollow jaguar (Plate XXVIII) were made. These three metals and their alloys continued to be the metals of choice for high-status use throughout the rest of Peruvian prehistory, though arsenic-bronze and tin-bronze ("true" bronze) were widely used after A.D. 800, and occasional use was made of lead, mercury, unalloyed tin, platinum, and meteoric iron.

SOURCES OF METALS

Gold could be, and still is today, gathered as flakes or nuggets of high purity from streams and rivers, particularly on the eastern slopes of the Andes mountains; on the coast, the greatest amount of placer gold is found in the Tumbes River of the far north (near the area of the early Vicus culture). However, much of the gold used in later times must have been mined, since the quantity we know of is so great. One of the early Spanish chroniclers reported that 6 million ounces of gold were produced annually under the Inca. The mining of gold was observed near La Paz, Bolivia, in 1534, before Spanish influence had radically altered the native pattern. The mines were worked only during the four warmest months of the year, and then only from noon until sunset, so as not to expose the miners to the harsh mountain cold. This concern for the miners is in marked contrast to the Spaniards, who decimated the Indian population in many areas by forcing them to work the mines under the most adverse conditions. But then, the Spanish had a very different view of gold and the mines than did the native. The Indian viewed the mines and ore-bearing hills as shrines (*huacas*), honoring them with dancing, toasting them with *chicha* (maize beer), and praying to their spirits to release the metals they held. The Spanish saw the mines simply as sources of wealth.

Copper and silver could also be found as native metals, though smelting them from ores was more common. Copper- and silver-bearing ores were widespread in Peru. The same was not true of tin, which alloyed with copper produces bronze; it was restricted to southern Peru, Bolivia, and northern Argentina, in the region south of Lake Titicaca. Until Peru was unified by the Inca, tin-bronze was used mainly in the south, near the tin mines. Prior to that time, bronzes made from alloys of arsenic and copper were widely used in the northern areas of Peru, and the shift from one alloy to the other coincides with the successful conquest of the Chimu state by the Inca, who for apparently political reasons instituted the use of tin-bronze throughout their empire.

56. One method of smelting metal used forced air from blowpipes to raise the temperature of the fire, as shown in this Moche ceramic bowl. Five men (one is missing) are shown around a circular adobe smelter, four blowing through long tubes while a fifth manipulates ingots and artifacts in the fire.

PROCESSING OF METALS

The smelting of mineral ores was accomplished by two principal means. One was the *huaira*, or wind furnace. These were cylindrical chimneys of masonry or pottery with many holes in their sides. They were set up on windy hillsides, filled with fuel and ore, and ignited. Wind blowing through the holes provided the draft necessary to raise the temperature of the fire high enough to smelt the ore. An early Spanish writer observed so many *huairas* being used in one area that their fires illuminated the hillside at night.

A second form of smelter used air blown through canes or tubes to create the draft. The ore (or metal, when it was being remelted for alloying or working) could be placed in a crucible or furnace, as shown in a Moche ceramic depiction (Figure 55), or placed in sleeves made of cloth plastered with mud and charcoal, as noted in Quito, Ecuador, the Inca's northern capital.

Most early studies of Peruvian metallurgy assumed that copper was smelted from its oxide and carbonate ores rather than from sulfide ores, a judgment based more on *a priori* considerations of technological "ease" or simplicity than on actual examination of artifacts or ores. Recent studies (Caley, 1973; Lechtman, 1976), however, indicate that sulfide ores, even though they required more complicated processing, were widely used in northern Peru. Thus, in this area Peruvian metallurgy was more advanced than many authorities were willing to concede.

Silver was smelted using galena (lead ore) or silver-rich lead ores in a process known as cupellation. In smelting and cupellation, the easily melted lead dissolves the silver and flows with it to the bottom of the smelter, where the mixture is drawn off. Repeated heatings of the lead-silver mixture cause the lead to oxidize, forming a film on the surface that can be skimmed off, leaving ever-more pure silver behind.

Tin used to make bronze was derived from cassiterite, its oxide ore. Cassiterite is easily smelted, and could be added to oxide or carbonate ores of copper, such as cuprite and malachite, and the two smelted directly to bronze. The ore cassiterite could also be added to copper and then smelted; or it could be smelted separately and then remelted with copper. The arsenic-bronze used by the Chimu in northern Peru was made by smelting ores that naturally contained both copper and arsenic.

The two bronzes—arsenic-copper bronze in the north and tin-copper bronze in the south—became the most widely used metals in Peru after about A.D. 1000. Bronze was used to make ornaments, weapons, and tools, in other words, for all types of objects, both hammered and cast. It was, in the words of one

expert, the Andean stainless steel, as widely used in ancient Peruvian society as the latter is used in our society.

Alloys of two or more metals have the advantage of melting at a lower temperature than their components, making them easier to cast in the low-temperature furnaces available to the Peruvians. An alloy is also often harder or more durable than its individual components. Pure gold is very soft and does not wear well without the addition of copper, for example. The properties of bronze vary with the amount of arsenic or tin in the alloy, and the Peruvian craftsmen were well aware of these differences. Alloys high in tin (about 10-13 per cent tin) cast easily and have good strength; low-tin bronze (about 5 per cent tin) is more suited to cold working, since it is ductile and less likely to become brittle when hammered. These two bronze alloys with their special properties were skillfully used by the native smith, who could forge the blade of a *tumi* knife from low-tin bronze, and then add on a molded handle with the more easily cast high-tin bronze.

Cold-hammered bronze, both arsenic and tin, can be as hard or harder than many types of iron, a fact overlooked by those who claim that the Inca's bronze tools were unsuited to working stone for their buildings. The same people who fault the Peruvians for not reaching an "Iron Age" also overlook differences in the cultural matrix in which the metals were used. A major impetus for the spread of iron in the Old World appears to have been iron's use in war, as a cutting sword or ax. Peruvian warfare depended on the sling, spear, and mace: swords were not used and knives, such as the *tumi*, appear often to have been as much ceremonial as functional. The Andean area lacked animals suitable for heavy work, such as plowing or pulling carts. Turning the soil was done with chisel-like foot plows, for which wood or bronze made eminently suitable points. Thus, many of the supposed advantages of iron were not relevant to the Andean cultural situation, and the Peruvians should not be faulted for not developing something that they did not need.

FORMING OF METALS

Peruvian metallurgy in general, and that of the coast in particular, is characterized by the use of cold-hammered sheet metal, especially in comparison to casting prevalent in Colombia or Central America. The Peruvian smiths hammered out large, flat, sheet objects, formed hollow three-dimensional figures, and raised deep seamless cups from single sheets which were often very thin and uniformly made. Their basic tools were small, smooth, hard stones used as hammer and anvil to slowly pound the ingots of metal into shape. Designs were added either by forming the piece in its final stage over a pattern or were done freehand with a stylus and resilient support.

When several pieces needed to be joined together, the native metal-worker had a variety of techniques at his disposal. Simplest was the use of wires, tabs, or rivets; more continuous joins were made using solder or welds. The hollow jaguar figure is very interesting in this respect. It is one of at least seven known, all the product of a single workshop, if not a single person. Studies on others of the set (Lechtman et al., 1975) have shown that each jaguar is composed of 12 pieces (not counting the bangles on the tail, which are found only on this jaguar): the upper and lower parts of the body and two halves each of the ears, front legs, and tail. These latter appendages were welded together, then soldered to the body. Different alloys were used at each stage, each increasingly easier to melt than the ones used earlier. Thus, the first joins would not remelt when the figure was reheated to make a subsequent join. The technique is well known to modern jewelers; this Peruvian example is about 2,000 years old.

Though not as common as cold hammering, casting was widely used with all types of metals. Casting was done in both open and closed molds, the latter often using the "lost-wax" method. In lost-wax casting, a model is first fashioned from wax or resin, coated with clay, and then baked, hardening the clay and melting away the wax model (hence the name "lost-wax"). The resulting void is then filled with molten metal, producing an exact copy of the model when the clay is broken away from the solidified casting. By this means very complicated or detailed objects can be made. The Inca appear to have

57. A *tumi* was a knife-like object with a flat, crescent-shaped blade and a long, perpendicular handle. Ornate specimens, such as this Chimu *tumi* with incised anthropomorphic figures, served ceremonial rather than utilitarian purposes.

58. Chimu metalsmiths excelled at forming sheet gold objects, such as this large mask, embossed from a single piece of alloy.

59. This small figure of embossed sheet gold wears a crescent-shaped headdress and circular ear spools characteristic of Chimu prestige apparel. He has upswept eye corners, a motif that appears on certain Huaca de la Luna murals and was later elaborated in the Lambayeque region.

made greater use of casting than did other Peruvian groups, though this conclusion may be biased by the results of looting.

Except for lead and fairly pure gold, which are extremely ductile, a metal becomes hard and brittle as it is cold hammered. In order to further hammer the piece, it must be heated to a high-enough temperature to release the stresses that have built up inside it. This process is called annealing. Since cold hammering hardens the metal, there are times when it is desirable not to anneal a piece, as after the final shaping of a knife or chisel, so that the edge retains this added hardness and durability.

Some alloys, such as the low-tin bronze mentioned above, were especially well suited to cold hammering. Another such alloy is the mixture of copper and silver, which produces extremely strong, thin sheets. Silver can occur in natural combination with native copper, or can be introduced by unintentionally smelting certain similar-looking ores, so this alloy could easily have been discovered accidentally. An important side effect of cold hammering and annealing a copper-silver alloy is that its surface becomes more and more silvery with each cycle, producing an appearance of pure silver automatically and unavoidably. This result was undoubtedly noted and imitated, since the earliest silver object we know of, dating to before 1000 B.C., is an intentional alloy of about half silver and half copper whose surface had been made to look like pure silver by this process, known as "depletion silvering." A similar result can be obtained using a gold-copper alloy. In this case, the process (similar to the Old World technique of "mise en couleur") is called "depletion gilding."

To depletion gild a piece, it is heated to oxidize ("rust") the copper at the surface, forming a black scale that can be removed by hammering or, more easily and with smoother results, by "pickling" (dissolving the copper oxide away with a weak acid). For this purpose, the smith could use certain acid plant juices, mineral soils, or even urine. As more and more copper was drawn to the surface and removed by repeated heatings and picklings, a layer of gold (which is resistant to most acids) would build up. This film could then be smoothed by burnishing or by heating it to fuse the surface.

Sometimes a ternary alloy of copper, silver, and gold—at times containing as little as 15 per cent gold—was used to make "gold" objects. Here the gilding process was a bit more complicated, as heating and pickling would remove the copper from the surface, but not the silver. To remove this silver, a paste of *salitre* (a soil high in mineral salts), alum, and common salt could be applied to the piece, heated, and removed, leaving the surface silver as a black scale that could be dissolved in a hot, strong, salt solution.

While depletion silvering and gilding might have been discovered as a side effect of hammering and annealing sheet metal, it is the heating, not the hammering, that is important. Thus, the process could also be used on cast objects. Depletion-gilded cast objects from Peru are known, but they are not as common there as in Colombia and Central America. Indeed, the process was so characteristic of Colombia that its native name for the gold-copper alloy, *tumbaga*, is applied to similar alloys from other areas of the New World as well.

Heather Lechtman, of the Massachusetts Institute of Technology, on whose experimental duplication of depletion gilding (Lechtman, 1973) the above discussion was based, has presented some interesting thoughts on the "why" as well as the "how" of Peruvian metallurgy. She argues that the use of alloys and depletion gilding was not principally a step to conserve gold: if this was the goal, then it could have been better achieved by using gold foil applied to the surface, a technique known to the ancient Peruvians but not commonly used. Also, since it is clear that many gold pieces were painted, hiding the gold, a simple conserving policy would have made these objects not of gold or gold alloy, but of copper or bronze.

Neither can the use of gold alloys and depletion gilding be entirely explained by technological considerations, for while the alloys are easier to melt and cast, and make the object harder than the pure metal alone, the same alloys were worked in widely different ways in different areas over a period of 3,000 years. Rather, Lechtman suggests that the basis of the continued use of gold alloys was that the incorporation of the "essence" of the object—in this case, its "goldness"—within it was essential, regardless of its final appearance. The "goldness" must come from within; a mere superficial coating would not do, even if the actual quantity of gold involved was the same.

The large Chimu mummy masks that look so golden were never seen. They were never seen, first, because their surfaces were covered with overlays of other metals, precious stones, and paint. The gold was invisible. Second, they were never seen because they were interred. Yet the masks had nevertheless to be of gold—to look golden—at least for those special persons for whom they were made. The essence had to be present though invisible.
(Lechtman, MS, p. 33).

Herein lies a key to understanding the different values applied to gold by the Peruvians and the Spaniards. The Spaniards saw gold as an *object* of value, a *thing* to be taken and hoarded, a thing of ultimate value. The Peruvians, on the other hand, saw value not so much in the gold itself as in the ideas it represented. Gold was more an object of social power than of economic power. Gold was not used as money; taxes were not paid in gold or some other physical commodity, but in labor. Fine cloth was as "valuable," if not more so, than gold, and certainly more obtainable for the average person. Gold was *the* metal of the Inca royalty, intimately associated with these divine descendants of the Sun. To them was reserved its possession. However, Pizarro and his band of Spaniards felt otherwise.

BIBLIOGRAPHY

General

Kosok, Paul
1965   *Life, Land and Water in Ancient Peru*. Long Island University Press, New York.

Lumberas, Luis G.
1974   *The Peoples and Cultures of Ancient Peru*. Smithsonian Institution Press, Washington, D.C.

Murra, John V.
1972   El "Control Vertical" de un maximo de pisos ecologicos en la economia de las sociedades andinas, pp. 429-476. *In:* Murra, J.V., editor, *Visita de la Provincia de Leon de Huanuco (1562)*, Volume II. Universidad Nacional Valdizan, Huanuco.

Inca

Brundage, Burr C.
1967   *Lords of Cuzco*. University of Oklahoma Press, Norman.

Cieza de León, Pedro de
1883   (1550) *Chronicle of Peru*. Markham, C.R., translator and editor, Hakluyt Society, London.

Murra, John V.
1962   Cloth and its functions in the Inca state. *American Anthropologist*, **64**, pp. 710-728.

Rowe, John H.
1946   Inca culture at the time of the Spanish Conquest. *In:* Steward, J.H., editor, *Handbook of South American Indians, Vol. 2*, pp. 183-330, Bureau of American Ethnology, Washington, D.C.

1967   What kind of settlement was Inca Cuzco? *Ñawpa Pacha*, **5**, pp. 59-77.

Chimu

Keatinge, Richard W., et al.
1975   From the sacred to the secular: first report on a prehistoric architectural transition on the north coast of Peru. *Archaeology*, **28**, pp. 128-129.

Moseley, Michael E.
1975   Chan Chan: Andean alternative of the preindustrial city. *Science*, **187**, pp. 219-225.

Rowe, John H.
1948   The kingdom of Chimor. *Acta Americana*, **6.**

Moche

Donnan, Christopher B.
1976   *Moche Art and Iconography*. UCLA Latin American Center Publications, University of California, Los Angeles.

Hastings, Charles M. and Michael E. Moseley
1975   The adobes of Huaca del Sol and Huaca de la Luna. *American Antiquity*, **40**, pp. 196-203.

Larco Hoyle, Rafael
1938-1939   *Los Mochicas*. Tomo I-II. Lima.

Moseley, Michael E.
1975   Prehistoric principles of labor organization in the Moche Valley, Peru. *American Antiquity*, **40**, pp. 191-196.

South Coast

Kroeber, Alfred L. and W. D. Strong
1924   *The Uhle Pottery Collections from Ica*. University of California Publications in American Archaeology and Ethnology, **21**, pp. 95-120.

Menzel, Dorothy, J. H. Rowe, and L. E. Dawson
1964   *The Paracas Pottery of Ica: A Study in Style and Time*. University of California Publications in America Archaeology and Ethnology, Vol. 50.

Prould, Donald A.
1970 *Nazca Gravelots in the Uhle Collection from the Ica Valley, Peru.* Research Reports, Department of Anthropology, University of Massachusetts, Number 5.

Roark, Richard Paul
1965 From monumental to proliferous in Nazca pottery. *Ñawpa Pacha*, **3**, pp. 1-92.

Reiche, Maria and Hermann Kern
1974 *Peruvian Ground Drawings*. Kunstraum Munchen e. V., Munchen.

Far North Coast

Disselhoff, Hans D.
1971 *Vicús: eine neu entdeckte alteperuansiche kultur.* Ibero-Amerikanischen Institut Preussischer Kulturbesitz. Gebr. Mann Verlag. Berlin.

Larco Hoyle, Rafael
1965 *La Ceramica de Vicús.* Lima.

Richardson, James B., III
1973 The prehistoric sequence and the Pleistocene and post-Pleistocene climate of northwest Peru, pp. 199-211. *In:* Lathrop, D. and J. Douglas, editors, *Variation in Anthropology*, Illinois Archaeological Survey.

Technology

Caley, Earle R.
1973 Chemical composition of ancient copper objects of South America, pp. 53-61. *In:* Young, W. J., editor., *Application of Science in Examination of Works of Art*, Museum of Fine Arts, Boston.

Donnan, Christopher B.
1973 A precolumbian smelter from northern Peru. *Archaeology*, **26**(4), pp. 289-297.

Grossman, Joel W.
1972 An ancient gold worker's tool kit: The earliest metal technology in Peru. *Archaeology*, **25**(4), pp. 270-275.

Lechtman, Heather N.
1973 The gilding of metals in precolumbian Peru, pp. 38-52. *In:* Young, W.J., editor, *Application of Science in Examination of Works of Art*, Museum of Fine Arts, Boston.

1976 A metallurgical site survey in the Peruvian Andes. *Journal of Field Archaeology*, **3**(1), pp. 1-42.

MS Issues in Andean metallurgy. Paper presented at the Conference on South American Metallurgy, Dumbarton Oaks, Washington, D.C., 18-19 October, 1975.

Lechtman, Heather N., Lee A. Parsons, and William J. Young
1975 *Seven Matched Hollow Gold Jaguars from Peru's Early Horizon*, Studies in Pre-Columbian Art and Archaeology, no. 16. Dumbarton Oaks, Trustees for Harvard University, Washington, D.C.

Lothrop, Samuel K.
1938 *Inca Treasure as Depicted by Spanish Historians*. Frederick Webb Hodge Anniversary Publication Funds, Vol. 2. Southwest Museum, Los Angeles.

1950-51 Metalworking tools from the central coast of Peru. *American Antiquity*, **16**(2), pp. 160-164.

Tushingham, A.D.
1976 Metallurgy. *In: Gold for the Gods*, a catalogue to an exhibition of pre-Inca and Inca gold and artifacts from Peru. Royal Ontario Museum, Toronto, pp. 55-64.